Project on Collecting Historic Data of Scientists' Academic Life Series
  Biography for Academicians at the Chinese Academy of Engineering Series

When Oil and Gas Meet the "Light"

A Biography of Zhai Guangming

Yan Jianwen

AMERICAN ACADEMIC PRESS

AMERICAN ACADEMIC PRESS

By AMERICAN ACADEMIC PRESS
201 Main Street
Salt Lake City
UT 84111 USA
Email manu@AcademicPress.us
Visit us at http://www.AcademicPress.us
Original Title: ◇◇◇◇◇◇◇◇◇◇

First published in China by China Science and Technology Press Co., Ltd. In 2017

Copyright © 2025 by AMERICAN ACADEMIC PRESS and ◇◇◇◇◇◇ (Petroleum Industry Press)

This English language edition is published by AMERICAN ACADEMIC PRESS under the license of Petroleum
Industry Press.

All rights reserved, including those of translation into foreign languages.

No part of this publication may be reproduced, stored in a retrieval system, or transmitted in any form or by any

means, electronic, mechanical, photocopying, recording, or otherwise, now known or hereafter invented, without

the prior written permission of the AMERICAN ACADEMIC PRESS, or as expressly permitted by law, or under

terms agreed with the appropriate reprographics rights organization. Enquiries concerning reproduction outside

the scope of the above should be sent to the Rights Department, American Academic Press, at the address

above.

The scanning, uploading, and distribution of this book via the Internet or via any other means without the

permission of the publisher is illegal and punishable by law. Please purchase only authorized editions and do not participate in or encourage electronic piracy of copyrighted materials. Your support of the publisher's right is appreciated.

ISBN: 979-8-3370-8951-5

Distributed to the trade by National Book Network Suite 200, 4501 Forbes Boulevard, Lanham, MD 20706

10 9 8 7 6 5 4 3 2 1

Expert Committee of the Leading Group of the Project on Collecting Historic Data of Scientists' Academic Life

Director: Du Xiang-wan

Committee Members (in alphabetical order by surname): Ba De-nian, Chen Jia'er, Hu Qi-heng, Li Zhen-sheng, Qi Rang, Wang Li-heng, Wang Chun-fa

Organization of the Project on Collecting Historic Data of Scientists' Academic Life Series

Special Consultants (in alphabetical order by surname): Fan Hong-ye, Fang Xin, Xie Ke-chang

Editorial Board Editors-in-Chief: Zhang Li, Wang Chun-fa

Editors (in alphabetical order by surname): Ai Su-zhen, Cui Yu-hong, Ding Yi-zhuang, Dong Qing-jiu, Guo Zhe, Han Jian-min, He Su-xing, Hu Hua-kai, Hu Zong-gang, Liu Xiao-kan, Luo Hui, Lü Rui-hua, Qin De-ji, Wang Ting, Wang Yang-zong, Xiong Wei-min, Yao Li, Zhang Da-qing, Zhang Jian, Zhou De-jin

Editorial Board Office Directors: Meng Ling-yun, Zhang Li-jie

Deputy Directors: Xu Hui

Members (in alphabetical order by surname): Liu Pei-ying, Dong Ya-zheng, Feng Qin, Gao Wen-jing, Han Ying, Li Mei, Liu Ru-xi, Luo Xing-bo, Shen Lin-qi, Tian Tian, Wang Chuan-chao, Yu Jun, Zhang Hai-xin, Zhang Jia-jing

Translator: Lai Tao

1

primary responsibility of the leading group is to provide guidance at the

of CAST and comprising leaders from 12 ministries and commissions. The

constituted at the inception of the Project, chaired by the principal leaders

the collection's standardization and scientific rigor, a leading group was

The Collecting Project represents a groundbreaking work. To guarantee

groundbreaking contributions.

career trajectories of these scientists and amplifying recognition of their

corpus furnishes raw archival evidence essential for examining the

in the academic careers of the scientists in question. This primary source

materials pertaining to the mentorship, significant moments and events

is to collate and conserve artifacts, oral history data and audio-visual

who are at an advanced stage of their professional careers. Its objective

Project is principally concerned with the academic development of scientists

and the National Natural Science Foundation of China are also involved. The

Academy of Sciences (CAS), the Chinese Academy of Engineering (CAE),

State Council, the General Political Department of the PLA, the Chinese

the State-owned Assets Supervision and Administration Commission of the

Technology. Additionally, the Ministry of Finance, the Ministry of Culture,

of Science and Technology, and the Ministry of Industry and Information

of the CPC Central Committee, the Ministry of Education, the Ministry

eleven ministries and commissions, including the Organization Department

Association for Science and Technology (CAST) in collaboration with

a rescue project, the Collecting Project is being implemented by the China

Leading Group with the endorsement of the leaders of the State Council. As

was officially inaugurated by the National Technology and Education

Life (hereinafter referred to as "the Collecting Project" or "the Project")

In 2010, the Project on Collecting Historic Data of Scientists' Academic

Academic Life
Collecting Historic Data of Scientists'
A Brief Introduction to the Project on

₂ evolution of China's scientific and technological endeavors.

the growth patterns of scientific and technological talents, and study the

public to gain insight into the remarkable journeys of senior scientists, trace

offering objective and comprehensive historical data that will enable the

continues to expand and evolve, a growing number of results will emerge.

biographies in collaboration with CAS and CAE. As the Collecting Project

the academic achievements of senior scientists, which are published as

format; and (3) the writing of research reports that objectively document

of documentary films featuring scientists, which are broadcast in video

contributions of Chinese scientists; (2) the editing and production of a series

academic research and disseminating information about the scientific

Scientists (web version), which serves the dual purpose of facilitating

categories: (1) the construction of the National Museum for Modern Chinese

The results of the Collecting Project can be broadly classified into three

exceptional historical significance.

video footage, and 4,963 hours audio recordings—a consolidated archive of

(including manuscripts and letters), 178,326 digitized objects, 4,037 hours of

been be in progress, resulting in the acquisition of 73,968 physical artifacts

2016, systematic documentation of over 400 senior scientists' careers had

Work Guidelines for the Collecting Project. By June and

Collecting Project Workflow for the

to serve as a reference for relevant personnel, including the

collected materials. Furthermore, a series of basic documents were developed

the objective of ensuring the long-term preservation and accessibility of the

organizational support. A dedicated collection base was established with

history of science were tasked with providing academic guidance and

furnish academic consultation. In addition, scholars specializing in the

pertinent principles, evaluate the list of academicians to be covered, and

an expert committee was appointed within the leading group to ascertain

macro level and to formulate important policies and measures. Concurrently,

3

conserving these materials in a way that reflects the significant moments and

oral history, audio-visual materials, and physical items, with the aim of

to collate a comprehensive and systematic collection of document literature.

The Collecting Project is conducted in a systematic manner. Its objective is

leading group since 2010.

growth data of veteran scientists has been organized and implemented by the

Natural Science Foundation of China. The project of collecting academic

(CAS), the Chinese Academy of Engineering (CAE), and the National

General Political Department of the PLA, the Chinese Academy of Sciences

Supervision and Administration Commission of the State Council, the

the Ministry of Finance, the Ministry of Culture, the State-owned Assets

and Technology, the Ministry of Industry and Information Technology,

Central Committee, the Ministry of Education, the Ministry of Science

and commissions, including the Organization Department of the CPC

CAST formed a leading group in collaboration with eleven ministries

Senior Scientists' Academic Life, which was approved by the State Council,

Plan for the Project on Collecting Historic Data of

In accordance with the

role and collaborate with relevant government departments to implement it.

of the State Council, who explicitly instructed CAST to assume a leading

materials. The proposal was met with considerable approval by the leaders

State Council in 2009, advocating for the preservation of the aged scientists'

Association for Science and Technology (CAST) presented a proposal to the

the concomitant loss of their invaluable academic materials, the China

issue of the untimely demise of quite a few scientists in recent years and

the historical development of these fields. In response to the significant

and education in modern China. It represents an integral component of

clear reflection of the progress made in the realms of science, technology,

country's scientific advancement. Their academic growth serves as a

Republic of China, serving as both contributors and observers in the

Senior scientists play a pivotal role in the development of the People's

General Preface I

by Han Qi-de, President of CAST

4

will be able to develop a more realistic understanding of scientists and their personalities of the older generation of scientists. Furthermore, young people profound insight into the accomplishments, contributions, experiences, and information, while the general public will gain a more systematic and will provide scholars with a more comprehensive and reliable source of of authenticity, professionalism, and readability. The series of biographies figures in a multifaceted manner, thereby achieving a harmonious synthesis immediacy of historical events. Concurrently, the biographies portray the images. These illustrations are comprehensive and compelling, capturing the invaluable photographic material, including manuscript copies and other rare meticulous textual analysis. Additionally, the collection includes a wealth of through the cross-verification of oral data and interviews, as well as through including archives and correspondence. This research is corroborated the foundation of comprehensive research into a multitude of documents. It is my assessment that the majority of these biographies are composed on

form of a biography, a goal that is widely anticipated by all sectors of society.

One of the primary objectives of the Project is to present the results in the

are some of great historical and academic value.

achievement among senior scientists. Among the materials in the collection

pertaining to the long and illustrious history of academic growth and

It has amassed a vast array of textual, physical, and audio-visual materials

for history, the country, and the advancement of science and technology.

of activities in accordance with the principle of assuming responsibility

Since its initiation in 2010, the Collecting Project has undertaken a series

scientists.

fully exemplifies the concern and care of the Party and the state for these

to other veteran scientists who have made significant contributions This

of age and have accumulated considerable academic experience, in addition

primary focus is on academicians of CAS and CAE who are over 80 years

social climate for the love, learning, and application of science. the Project

selfless dedication among sci-tech workers, and the creation of a favorable

tech talents, the promotion of the spirit of truth-seeking, pragmatism and

of the laws governing the development of sci-tech and the growth of sci-

the context of academic inheritance within sci-tech circles, the exploration

to the development of science and technology (sci-tech), the clarification of

of great significance for the enrichment of historical documents pertaining

education, mentorship, research activities, and academic achievements. It is

events in the academic careers of the senior scientists. This will include their

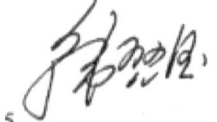   This serves as the preface.

become increasingly significant in the eyes of the wider world.

disseminated in a variety of formats. It is also expected that the Project will

passage of time, the Project will yield further results and that these will be

receive more extensive attention and support. It is anticipated that, with the

academic community and appreciated by readers, and that the Project will

my sincere hope that this series of biographies will be recognized by the

as to the staff and departments involved in the collection process. It is

their relatives, and friends who have participated in the Project, as well

I would like to express my sincerest gratitude to all the senior scientists,

science.

scientific activities, which may stimulate their interest in pursuing a career in

6

of scientists within their respective disciplines. It also assists the discovery

People's Republic of China, particularly in relation to the growth and success

conducive to a deeper understanding of the development of science in the

and the development background of relevant disciplines. The Project is

be examined in conjunction with the social development at different times

academic development of these scientists. Furthermore, the materials will

illuminate pivotal events and junctures, and mentoring relationships in the

of a range of documents, physical materials, and audio-visual content that

by all. The Project will enable the systematic collection and organization

emergence of a society where science is embraced, studied, and utilized

and creativity among sci-tech professionals, ultimately contributing to the

the People's Republic of China. Moreover, it aims to foster innovation

development, and to facilitate the formation of an academic tradition within

is to augment the historical data pertaining to the scientific and technological

recording and the physical collection of materials. Additionally, the objective

achieved through a range of methods, including the use of audio and video

the history of the academic advancement of senior scientists. This will be

objective of the Project is to preserve significant materials that document

Senior Scientists' Academic Life, approved by the State Council, the principal

Plan for the Project on Collecting Historic Data of

In accordance with the

express my sincerest gratitude to the senior scientists and staff involved.

warmest congratulations on the successful implementation of the Project and

biography series of the Collecting Project, I would like to extend my

and technological community. On the occasion of the publication of the

the State Council and a pivotal occurrence within the Chinese scientific

Academy of Sciences (CAS). It is a significant responsibility entrusted by

China Association for Science and Technology (CAST) and the Chinese

and jointly organized by 12 departments and commissions, including the

directly initiated by the National Technology and Education Leading Group

The Project on Collecting Historic Data of Scientists' Academic Life was

General Preface II

by Bai Chun-li, President of CAS

and society. The creation of biographies for these distinguished scientists the People's Republic of China, but also valuable assets for the country not only a microcosm of the scientific and technological development of academic achievements and growth experiences of these scientists represent instrumental role in the advancement of the scientific spirit and ideas. The contributions to the cultivation of young talents, thereby playing an security. As outstanding science educators, they have made noteworthy and social development, scientific and technological progress, and national innovation, and have made remarkable contributions to China's economic demonstrated a commitment to truth-seeking, pragmatism, pioneering, and serving the nation, and enhancing the well-being of the populace. They have leaders, they assume the responsibility of advancing science and technology, careers to advancing their specialized disciplines. As esteemed academic their fields of study, and distinguished scholars who have dedicated their fields, renowned scientists who have made significant contributions to

individuals who were instrumental in the development of their respective

of CAS who were elected in the 1980s and 1990s. The group includes

have participated in the Project to date are members and academicians

of science in China. A significant proportion of the senior scientists who

period has been marked by significant contributions to the advancement

structure as divisions to its current status as an academy of sciences. This

challenging process of institutional development, evolving from its original

of CAS. Over the course of more than half a century, CAS has undergone a

CAS, and in 1993, the State Council decided to rename them academicians

As early as 1955, the first members of academic divisions were elected by

of academicians.

collective for the unification and integration of a vast number

team for the advancement of science and technology, but also as a significant

The Chinese Academy of Sciences (CAS) serves not only as the national

endeavor.

a cultural project, but also a serious and earnest academic construction

of science and innovation. In this sense, the Collecting Project is not only

in the whole society. This will promote the development of socialist culture

thoughts, outstanding contributions, and noble qualities of these scientists

process of Chinese scientific tradition, and publicizing the scientific

inheritance in China's scientific community, understanding the formation

Most importantly, it is instrumental in clarifying the context of academic

the training of high-level talents and the growth of innovative talents.

success, as well as the exploration and comprehension of the laws governing

of key figures, events and factors that have shaped their development and

8   nation.

thereby propelling China towards its aspiration of becoming an innovative

extensive trajectory of advancing scientific and technological advancement,

so, they will undoubtedly achieve more remarkable outcomes along the

cooperation, and a dedication to serving the motherland and society. In doing

scientific spirit of pursuing truth and excellence, the team spirit of unity and

qualities of the senior scientists, and that they will continue to exemplify the

biography series will inspire the sci-tech workers to emulate the admirable

be written by the scientists of today. It is hoped that the reading of this

preceding older generation of scientists, and a new chapter of history will

glorious history of the past has been shaped by the contributions of the

"ascend beyond the heights reached by the predecessors." Similarly, the

In his writings, Lu Xun observed that it was imperative for individuals to

contributions, as well as to fulfill a long-held aspiration.

through the Collecting Project serves to commend their achievements and

9

The remarkable accomplishments of these initiatives can be attributed

motherland.

for the vigorous development of the socialist cause and the prosperity of the

supercomputers, each of these major projects has written a splendid chapter

speed railways, the manned space program, hybrid rice, manned deep diving,

Bombs, One Satellite" Project to the Three Gorges Project, and to high-

considerably to the modernization of the motherland. From the "Two

and technicians have made great historic achievements and contributed

the past 30 years of reform and opening up, our engineers, scientists

Since the founding of the People's Republic of China, especially over

the pursuit of scientific and technological endeavors.

pivotal role in the advancement of scientific and technological progress and

forces and disseminators of advanced culture, scientists and engineers play a

economic and social development. As pioneers of advanced productive

productive force, has increasingly become the principal driving force for

In the contemporary historical period, science and technology, as the primary

knowledge.

holds great significance for the advancement of scientific and technological

significant responsibility entailed in participating in this activity, which

Project, the Chinese Academy of Engineering (CAE) recognizes the

China as a whole. As a member unit of the leading group of the Collecting

Furthermore, this is a responsibility shared by the scientific community in

technological experts and to strengthen the construction of scientific ethics.

purpose is to promote the lofty spirit of the older generation of scientific and

an important mission that has been approved by the State Council. Its

Science and Technology (CAST) and other relevant departments, represents

which is jointly organized and implemented by the Chinese Association for

The Project on Collecting Historic Data of Scientists' Academic Life,

by Zhou Ji, President of CAE **General Preface III**

10

community and society at large to preserve the academic growth experiences

obligation, and the shared expectation of the scientific and technological

veteran experts in the fields of science and technology. It is our aspiration,

brought together a substantial cohort of highly accomplished and respected

in China's engineering and science and technology community. It has

CAE is the most esteemed honorary and consultative academic institution

innovation and the application of scientific knowledge.

in turn, will foster a scientific ethos that encourages a culture of learning,

the admirable qualities and spirit exemplified by these individuals. This,

to younger scientists and engineers, enabling them to learn from and emulate

scientific advancement and national development. This will provide guidance

to disseminate information about their invaluable contributions to China's

will edit and publish their academic biographies. It is of great significance

outstanding technical achievements and valuable spiritual qualities, and it

academic growth of senior scientists. Additionally, the Project records their

of significant textual, physical, and audio-visual materials that reflect the

The implementation of the Collecting Project will lubricate the preservation

generations.

qualities are worthy of enduring remembrance and admiration by future

demonstrate the Chinese people's spirit of relentless self-betterment. These

to their ideals, unflinching integrity, and indifference to worldly accolades

invaluable source of insight and inspiration. Their unwavering commitment

as exemplars for future generations. The lives of scientists provide an

pursuits, manifesting a profound scientific ethos and ethical conduct, serving

They were meticulous in their studies and dedicated to their professional

technology that contributed to the great rejuvenation of the Chinese nation.

innovative, attaining impressive advancements in the field of science and

enhance the country's prosperity and strength. They were pragmatic and

careers into the broader framework of national development, striving to

patriotic sentiments and loyalty to the people, integrating their individual

striving to promote innovative development. They showed profound

those related to technology, conducting rigorous scientific research, and comprehensive strength by overcoming numerous challenges, particularly of Chinese engineering technologies and the enhancement of national ping. They made significant contributions to the exceptional advancement Xue-sen, Zhu Guang-ya, Zhou Guang-zhao, Hou Xiang-lin, and Yuan Long- scientific and technological experts, exemplified by figures such as Qian to the unwavering commitment and innovative spirit of generations of

11 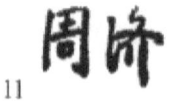 People's Republic of China.

and contribute a valuable data set to the scientific advancement of the

inspire future generations, provide a foundation of knowledge for society,

of these distinguished individuals in a variety of formats. This will serve to

12 Zhai Guangming (Photo by Yu Hang in 2014)

13 (From left: Yan Jianwen, Zhai Guangming, Wang Duan. Photo by Yu Hang)

The collection team discussing with academician Zhai Guangming.

left: Zhai Guangming, Wan Yan. Photo by Yu Hang)

(Back row from left: Yang Xian-yi, Li Fen, Wang Duan, Yan Jianwen, Liu ; Front row from

The collection team verifying the data with academician Zhai Guangming.

14

and archives. The team employed a variety of methods, including literature

efforts to engage with all relevant individuals to obtain a range of documents

demonstrating a sense of personal responsibility, and undertook meticulous

preparation of the report. collection team operated in a collaborative manner,

A comprehensive plan was devised for the collation of data and the

comprising members from the Publicity Department of the Party Committee.

collection team was established under the guidance of RIPED leadership,

great importance to it and provided substantial assistance. In particular, a

of Petroleum Exploration & Development (RIPED) of CNPC attached

China National Petroleum Corporation (CNPC) and the Research Institute

(BAST), as well as the Ideological and Political Work Department of

Technology (CAST), the Beijing Association for Science and Technology

During the collection process, the Chinese Association for Science and

historical documents for the study and reference of future generations.

petroleum industry with a substantial corpus of reliable and informative

petroleum exploration in China and to furnish the development of China's

and obligation to provide an account of the history of the development of

a subject for the Project in 2013. I have considered it my responsibility

I have been greatly honored and delighted to learn that I was selected as

energizing the nation's journey toward rejuvenation.

This intellectual heritage will perpetually inspire future generations.

Scientific Dream & Chinese Dream: Legacy of Modern Chinese Scientists.

asset. These results will also serve as a core component of the exhibition

and innovative thinking of these scientists, represent a significant intellectual

repository. The findings of the Project, particularly the academic insights

brilliant achievements created by them to be brought together in a single

history of endeavor and entrepreneurship of the senior scientists and the

the annals of Chinese science and technology. The Project has enabled the

pertaining to many academicians, constituting a significant milestone in

Scientists' Academic Life has yielded a substantial corpus of materials

Since its inception in 2010, the Project on Collecting Historic Data of

Preface

15

my pursuit of oil and gas. Over the past six decades, I have been privileged

up to 12,000 meters. Upon graduating from college in 1950, I commenced

ability to operate in a multitude of complex terrains and to drill to depths of

drilling. The current state of the art in seismic exploration encompasses the

of supporting technologies, including seismic exploration and deep well

The process of exploring the underground world is dependent on a range

earth", entails probing deep strata to search for oil, gas, water, and minerals.

goal. The exploration of the subterranean environment, or "down into the

demonstrate that the exploration of outer space is no longer an unattainable

has landed on the Moon and moved around its surface. These achievements

space, the Chang'e lunar probes are orbiting the Moon, and the Yutu rover

technology. The Shenzhou manned spacecraft is currently probing deep

the exploration of the cosmos dependent on the advancement of space

Earth. Accessing space represents a long-held aspiration of humanity, with

process of ascending to outer space and descending into the depths of the

acknowledged that the most challenging aspect of exploration is the repeated practice can a higher success rate be achieved. It is commonly research and resolute, well-founded scientific judgement. It is only through scientific principles. It necessitates comprehensive on-site geological and practical knowledge, as well as a willingness to take risks based on and gas exploration is a field that requires a close integration of theoretical my life with a rich tapestry of experiences in the finding of oil and gas. Oil petroleum Exploration & Development. These occurrences have imbued triumphs and setbacks, positive and negative emotions, in the field of historical events and underwent a range of outcomes, including both emotions. In the course of my career, I have witnessed the evolution of Looking back on my 90 years of life's journey, I am filled with countless spirit of the team members and their tireless efforts to the Project.
have put forth. I am deeply impressed by the scientific attitude and pragmatic theoretical and methodological frameworks for oil and gas exploration that I essentially encapsulates my academic growth trajectory and synthesizes the

and select contributions to the field of oil and gas exploration in China. It

meticulously delineating my familial background, academic trajectory,

Based on this, the team promptly drafted an academic biography,

long-buried memories, thereby enabling the portrayal of my life experiences.

restoration of the original context of historical events and the evocation of

materials and information related to me. These methods facilitated the

artifact collection, and retracing key venues, to identify and retrieve

reviews, thematic interviews, personal interviews, telephone interviews.

16

has demonstrated remarkable dedication, devoting almost all of his personal

of RIPED, the author of the biography. Over the past three years, Dr. Yan

I would be remiss if I did not also express my gratitude to Dr. Yan Jianwen

my conviction in the feasibility of the Chinese Dream.

future with greater color and infinite strength. Furthermore, it has reinforced

and once again reached a new pinnacle in my life, which has imbued my

understanding of myself, synthesized my ideas, augmented my knowledge,

to their selfless dedication and assiduous efforts that I have gained a deeper

been feasible without the full support of the aforementioned parties. It is due

team. The achievement of such a rich collection of results would not have

financial support and assistance, as well as to each member of the research

my gratitude to RIPED of CNPC for its invaluable human, material, and

family members for their support and assistance. I would like to extend

High School, and Peking University; to my classmates, colleagues, and

my alma mater, including Tianjin Muzhai Middle School, Beijing No. 1

all levels of CNPC and SINOPEC, as well as affiliated oil companies; to

I would like to express my gratitude to CAST, BAST, the leadership at

energy security.

thereby contributing to the search for oil and gas and maintaining national

will continue to utilize my remaining energy to the fullest extent possible,

further oil and gas reserves will be discovered and explored in the future. I

a meaningful contribution to my field of expertise. It is anticipated that

I feel a sense of pride and gratitude, and I am also pleased to have made

have a profound emotional attachment to this substance. Consequently,

history of petroleum has always held a special significance for me, and I

the territory where oil and gas discoveries have been made in China. The

can be stated that my activities have been conducted across the entirety of

the deserts in Xinjiang, and from the inland basins to the offshore areas. It

Songliao Basin to the Bohai Bay Basin, from the gas region in Sichuan to

Yumen Oilfield to the Ministry of Petroleum Industry in Beijing, from the

I have observed the evolution of China's oil and gas industry, from the

in the strategic research of China's oil and gas as a planner and participant.

Shengli, Huabei, Changqing and Tuha. Furthermore, I have been engaged

and discovery of a multitude of oil and gas fields, including Daqing,

Sea. I have been a witness, participant and practitioner of the exploration

Gansu-Ningxia, Jianghan, Turpan-Hami (Tuha), Tarim, and the South China

exploration campaigns in Sichuan, Songliao, North China (Huabei), Shaanxi-

to observe the evolution of China's petroleum industry, contributing to oil

17 2016 March, Zhai Guangming

This is the conclusion of the preface. of this Collecting Project.

I would like to express my sincerest gratitude for the successful completion

style.

time to the Project and completing the manuscript with a simple yet effective

General Preface III *by Bai Chunli*

Preface *by Zhou Ji* ....

Introduction ....
....*by Zhai Guangming*

1

....**Chapter 1 A Rootless Childhood**

....**Chapter 2 Tireless Learning Despite Difficulties** 7

....2.1 Tianjin Huiwen Elementary School 14

....2.2 Tianjin Muzhai Middle School 15

....2.3 Beiping No. 1 High School 16

2.4 Geology Department at Peking University 20

...............**Chapter 3 Bonding with Oil Exploration in the Northwest**

3.1 Going to the Northwest 45

3.2 Geological Expedition in the Northwest 47

3.3 Oil Exploration at Silangmiao in Northern Shaanxi 53

CONTENTS

General Preface II ....

....*by Han Qide*

General Preface I Scientists' Academic Life

A Brief Introduction to the Project on Collecting Historic Data of

When Oil and Gas Meets the "Light": A Biography of Zhai Guangming

Chapter 6 Leading the Research Institute of Petroleum Exploration & Development (RIPED) 194

6.1 Entry into the RIPED 194

6.2 Formulating Scientific and Technological Development Plan of RIPED 195

6.3 Participating in Oilfield Exploration & Development Practice 200

6.4 Deepening the Reform of the Scientific and Technological System 203

6.5 Opening up the Jidong Experimental Field 208

6.6 Conducting Research at the RIPED 210

6.7 The RIPED of Today 218

Chapter 7 Advocating for Scientific Exploration Wells 225

5.8 Major Achievements in Oil Exploration Campaigns in the South China Sea 182

5.7 The Geophysical Exploration Campaign in 177

5.6 The Oil Exploration Campaign in Lower Liaohe 168

5.5 The Oil Exploration Campaign in Shaanxi-Gansu-Ningxia 145

.... 5.4 The Oil Exploration Campaign in North China 124

5.3 The Oil Exploration Campaign in the Songliao Basin 110

.... 5.2 The Oil Exploration Campaign in Central Sichuan 107

5.1 The Eve of the Campaigns .... 106 ...

Chapter 5 Participating in Major Oilfield Exploration Campaigns

.... 98 4.2 Reporting to Deng Xiaoping at Zhongnanhai

.... 93 4.1 Entry into the Ministry of Petroleum Industry 92

.... **Chapter 4 From Yumen to Beijing**

.... 74 3.4 Yumen Oilfield Development and Construction

................................348 and Pipeline Development Strategies

11.4 Presiding over the Study on National Oil and Gas Supply 338....

11.3 Proposing Ten Breakthroughs in Oil and Gas Exploration 329

.... Development Strategies

11.2 Reporting to Premier Wen Jiabao on Sustainable Energy

................................323 11.1 Facing the Energy Dilemma in the 21st Century

....321

Security...

Chapter 11 Being Committed to National Oil and Gas Energy 315

....10.2 Footprints Across the World 303........

10.1 Introducing the World Petroleum Congress to China

...........................301

Chapter 10 International Exchanges and Cooperation 296...........

9.2 The Third National Oil and Gas Resource Appraisal 289........

9.1 The Second National Oil and Gas Resource Appraisal 288

Chapter 9 Hosting the National Oil and Gas Resource Appraisal 286

Chapter 8 Organization and Completion of Theoretical Writings on Petroleum Geology 275

8.1 Leading the Compilation of the Series *Petroleum Geology of China* .... of China

8.2 The Practice and Application of Plate Tectonics 277

8.3 Editing the monograph *Petroleum Geology of China* 284

7.1 Proposing the Scientific Exploration Well Program

7.2 The Well Taican-1: The First Spring Flower 227 ....

7.3 Discovery of the Well Shaancan-1 231

7.4 Extensions of Scientific Exploration Wells 248

7.5 Management Experience of Scientific Exploration Wells 259

7.6 The Core Value and Significance of the 262 ....

273 .... Scientific Exploration Well Program

489

Afterword ....

468 ....

Bibliography 466

Mentor Zhai Guangming on His 80th Birthday ....

Appendix III: A Congratulatory Letter from Xu Feng yin to His 456

.... Monographs

Appendix II : A Catalogue of Zhai Guangming's Major Works 411

Appendix I: The Chronology of Zhai Guangming ....

408 ....

Concluding Remarks: An Epilogue with No Real Ending 405

.... 13.5 Innermost Words from the Academician 394

.... 13.4 Light of Thoughts 385 ..

13.3 Comprehensive Exploration Work Methods of Oil and Gas 375

.... the Dialectical Relationships

13.2 Division of Oil and Gas Exploration Stages and 371 ....

11.5 Conducting Geological Research on Block Oil and Gas Exploration ....

Chapter 12 Master's Demeanor and Fruitful Achievements 353

12.1 Elected as an Academician of Chinese 356
.... Academy of Engineering

.... 12.2 Fruitful Achievements and Honors 357

12.3 Staying Attuned to Petroleum Education and 359
362 .... Society Organizations

Chapter 13 Philosophical Thoughts on Oil and Gas Exploration 370

13.1 A Review of Oil and Gas Exploration Practices

and created the CSI oil and gas exploration methodology, making indelible

proposed and implemented the planning of scientific exploration wells,

histories" of oil-bearing basins and the formation of oil-bearing basins,

of oil and gas geology such as the comprehensive analysis of "three

in all the "Oil Battles", or Oil Exploration Campaigns, put forward theories

including Daqing, Shengli, Changqing, Huabei and Liaohe. He participated

formulation and implementation of exploration plans for major oil regions,

and organized its implementation. He organized and participated in the

formulation of the water injection development plan for Laojunmiao Oilfield

the China Association for Science and Technology. He participated in the

of the CPS, and a Standing Committee member of the third session of

Executive Director of the first session and Director of the second session

of the 15th WPC, Vice Chairman of the 33rd session of the GSC, the

member of the Chinese National Committee of the WPC, Secretary-General

member of the Executive Board of the World Petroleum Congress (WPC), the Circum-Pacific Council for Energy and Mineral Resources (CPCEMR),

Honorary Director of the Geological Society of China (GSC), Director of

Society (CPS), Director of the Petroleum Geology Committee of the CPS,

Sinica, Vice Chairman and Executive Director of the Chinese Petroleum

Acta Petrolei

of CNPC. He also served as Editor-in-Chief of the periodical

CNPC and Deputy Director of the Expert Committee of the Advisory Center

(CNPC), Director of the Exploration Section of the Advisory Center of

Exploration & Development of China National Petroleum Corporation

of Petroleum Industry, Director of the Research Institute of Petroleum

and Director of the Geological Exploration Department of the Ministry

positions including Chief Geologist of the Yumen Oil Mine, Chief Geologist

and was elected as an academician of CAE in 1995. He once held various

He graduated from the Geology Department at Peking University in 1950

in October 1926, with ancestral roots in Jingxian County, Anhui Province.

petroleum geological exploration. He was born in Yichang, Hubei Province

Zhai Guangming (*the given name literally means "light"*), academician of the Chinese Academy of Engineering (CAE), is a well-known expert in

Introduction

2

Beijing', Zhai was transferred to the Ministry of Petroleum Industry (MPI) & development at the Yumen Oilfield. In Chapter Four, 'From Yumen to exploration at Silangmiao in Northern Shaanxi, as well as the exploration he went to the Northwest to participate in the geological survey and the oil of his journey in oil exploration. As soon as he graduated from university, 'Bonding with Oil Exploration in the Northwest', depicting the initial stage as well as changes in the social environment. Chapter Three is about Zhai's Beiping No. 1 High School and Geology Department of Peking University, at Tianjin Huiwen Elementary School, Tianjin Muzhai Middle School, narrates Zhai's life and learning as a student, including his study experience nomadic childhood. Chapter Two, 'Tireless Learning Despite Difficulties', Rootless Childhood', tracks the root of Zhai Guangming's family and his the oil and gas exploration in China's petroleum industry. Chapter One, 'A Zhai's life along the trajectory of his academic growth and the course of detail, depicting its original state. It also portrays a brilliant picture of contributions. The biography strives to accurately review the history in background, the course of events, and his personal role and historical one by one, like peeling an onion, from multiple angles, including historical unfolding according to that topic. It describes Zhai Guangming's life events several sections. Each section describes a specific topic, with the narrative The book is divided into thirteen chapters, each of which is subdivided into and benefit the society.

academic thoughts and historical contributions to inspire future generations context of the development of China's petroleum industry, summarizing his of the biography, it has outlined the course of Zhai's academic career in the of events. After thoroughly studying all the materials about the protagonist compared each piece of information to verify the time nodes and the course on special topics. During this process, the team carefully analyzed and audio-visual materials, and conducted more than 30 interviews with Zhai including almanacs, chronicles, biographies, personal memoirs, letters, and Moreover, it consulted many historical materials in petroleum and geology,

and development of his scientific methodology and academic thoughts.

Zhai's schooling experience, his practice of oil exploration, the generation

collection, interviews and research on academic materials centering on

research as thread, the team carried out various tasks, including data

academic growth of academician Zhai Guangming. Taking his academic

In 2013, the research team undertook the task of collecting materials on the

contributions to China's oil and gas exploration.

3

an academician of the CAE, reviews his fruitful achievements and honorary
and Fruitful Achievements', sketches Zhai's experience of being elected as
of oil and gas exploration of blocks. Chapter Twelve, 'Master's Demeanor
pipeline development strategy, and his pioneering research on the geology
exploration, his leadership in the research on national oil and gas supply and
sustainable energy strategy, his proposal of ten breakthroughs in oil and gas
dilemma in the 21st century, his report to Premier Wen Jiabao on the
Oil and Gas Energy Security', illustrates his contemplation on the energy
travels and harvest overseas. Chapter Eleven, 'Being Committed to National
China and his contributions, recording his footprints around the worldwide
Cooperation', it mainly portrays the process of Zhai introducing the WPC to
and gas resource evaluation. In Chapter Ten, 'International Exchanges and
and the important achievements of Zhai in the second and third national oil
and Gas Resource Appraisal', mainly introduces the research processes
Petroleum Geology of China. Chapter Nine, 'Hosting the National Oil

and

Petroleum Geology of China, Practice and Application of Plate Tectonics

Annals of

Geology'. It reports Zhai's achievements in the compilation of

about 'Organization and Completion of Theoretical Writings on Petroleum

management experience of scientific exploration wells. Chapter Eight is

as well as the extension of scientific exploration wells, summarizing the

Zhai, focusing on the discovery of Well Taican-1 and Well Shaancan-1,

Wells', it details the planning of scientific exploration wells proposed by

In Chapter Seven, 'Advocating for Petroleum Scientific Exploration

field, and conducting research and implementing various research work.

production consortium, opening up the Jidong (Eastern Hebei) experimental

the reform of scientific and technological system, establishing a research and

participating in the practice of oilfield exploration & development, deepening

the institute: formulating the scientific and technological development plan,

initial arrival at the institute. Additionally, it chronicles his various work at

(RIPED)', records the difficulties and challenges faced by Zhai upon his 'Leading Research Institute of Petroleum Exploration & Development finally recaps the major achievements of these campaigns. Chapter Six, Shaanxi-Gansu-Ningxia, the Lower Liaohe, and the South China Sea, and exploration campaigns in central Sichuan, Songliao Basin, North China, eve of the campaign, and then highlights his participation in the petroleum Campaigns', is a key chapter in this book. It first tells the preparations on the future career. Chapter Five, 'Participating in Major Oilfield Exploration which increased his confidence in finding oil and pointed the way to his to Deng Xiaoping, then General Secretary of PRC, in Zhongnanhai, and participated in a report on the development of the petroleum industry

4

been garnered, including theses, publications, seminar photos, discussion

the comprehensive oil and gas exploration method invented by Zhai have

Third, the materials on the background, development and improvement of

historical truth.

materials from the parties involved, providing evidence for clarifying the

designs, and evaluation reports. There are also a bunch of memoirs and oral

documents, handwritten notes, telex originals, photographs, program

have been collected, including meeting minutes, leadership approval

in the 1980s and the final discovery of Well Taican-1 and Well Shaancan-1

implementation and evaluation of the "scientific exploration well" program

Second, more than 30 documents related to the proposal, decision-making,

of the Daqing Oilfield, with important historical value.

most powerful first-hand materials related to the discovery and development

makers, implementers, and specific indicators of the plans, making them the

sandstone oilfields. The diaries clearly record the proposers, decision

determined the extraction mode for the development of China's multilayered

improvement and final decision-making process of the plans, which

put forward by different experts at that time, as well as the modification,

they recount the prototype of three sets of experimental development plans

the earliest of its kind of the People's Republic of China. Most importantly,

chronicle the exploration & development process of the Daqing Oilfield,

First, more than 20 diaries of Zhai in the 1960s have been collected, which

collected.

& development in China. There are mainly six important items of materials

historical status and achievements in the process of petroleum exploration

petroleum industry in China. These materials have fully proven Zhai's

the study of the history of petroleum exploration & development, and of

items of great historical value, providing first-hand material evidence for

During the collection process, the team has obtained numerous important

light of his thinking and his innermost words as an academician.

working method put forth by Zhai Guangming, with a recapitulation of the

and their dialectical relations, and the comprehensive oil and gas exploration

gas exploration, fixating on the division of stages in oil and gas exploration

Thoughts on Oil and Gas Exploration', briefly reviews the practice of oil and

titles, displaying the master's demeanor. In Chapter Thirteen, 'Philosophical

5 cultivate future talents.

future generations to achieve their full potential, as well as recognize and

dialectical manner, the biography serves as a reference and guidance for

growth trajectory. By examining the scientist's strengths in a historical and

on the scientist's unique and personal approach to scholarship and academic

economic development. Furthermore, it analyzes the impact of these factors

exchanges, the development of the oil and gas industry, and the national

professional expertise in oil and gas exploration, international academic

his family background, educational experiences, mentoring relationships,

development path of the entire petroleum industry in China. It chronicles

achievements, taking into account the historical background and the

The biography accurately recounts Zhai Guangming's academic

the overall situation of the country's resources.

China, and reflecting the development stages of the petroleum industry and

demonstrating the results of previous evaluation of oil and gas resources in

in China have been compiled, including evaluation methods and reports,

Sixth, the literature materials on the evaluation of oil and gas resources

the reform of today's scientific research system.

technology system have been amassed, which still have reference value for

research and production consortium in the reform of petroleum science and

Fifth, the documentary sources of Zhai's innovative proposal to establish a

petroleum community.

entire process of China's enhanced discourse power in the international

preparation, presiding over the congress, and other activities, showing the

and conference documents during the application process, organization and

gathered, including photos, speeches, central committee approval documents,

exchanges and striving for the 15th WPC to be held in China have been

Fourth, textual materials related to Zhai's participation in international

research on the formation of this comprehensive method.

records and other original materials, providing favorable evidence for further

Chapter 1
A Rootless Childhood

9 *Root Exploration*, 2002 (2), pp. 46-49. of Jingxian County,

Yongkang, Famous Families of the South of the Yangtze River: The Zhai Clan Chen

[2] Collecting Project Database.

Zhai Guangming Interview, September 17, 2013, Beijing: Materials stored in the

[1] _____ [2] county examination), (scholars who passed the *xiucai*

provincial examination), and one thousand (scholars who passed the

passed the palace examination), one hundred *juren* (scholars who

(member of the Imperial Academy), eleven *jinshi hanlin* six

generations of illustrious figures who have achieved widespread fame, including

Jingxian Annals, there were successive and

Ningguo Prefectural Records

therefore, spreads far and wide across the land." According to the Genealogy,

officialdom, and their lineage has continued for several generations. Their fame,

ascended to high ranks in the imperial examinations, joined the prestigious

individuals and outstanding heroes, emerging in large numbers. They have

of cultivation and the advent of civilization, they have produced auspicious

region, has accumulated wisdom and virtue over generations. With a long history also states, "The Zhai family of Shuidong in Jingxian, a prominent clan in the flourishing literary writings and the abundance of talents. From the preface, it world." Apart from that, the Zhai clan of Shuidong became famous also for its in his poem To Wang Lun, the name of Shuidong was heard throughout the behind a famous line as 'However deep the Lake of Peach Blossoms may be' his friend Wang Lun from Peach Blossoms Lake at Shuidong Village, leaving 220 CE). However, after Li Bai, a poet in the Tang Dynasty (618-907), visited world. Nothing was heard of this place before the Han Dynasty (206 BCE- by top mountain ranges and deep valleys, as if separated from the rest of the there is a village called Shuidong, where the Zhai clan resides, surrounded of the Ming Dynasty (1368-1644) reads, "Eighty miles southwest of Jingxian, Zhai Clan Genealogy of Shuidong in the reign of Emperor Jiajing (1522-1566) well as one of the most prestigious clans in southern Anhui. The preface to the The Zhai clan of Shuidong village is one of the major surnames in Jingxian as Zhai Guangming's ancestral home is in Jingxian County, Anhui Province.[1]

Chapter 1 A Rootless Childhood

10

memory and to commemorate the National Day, which has been used to this day.

solar calendar, he later changed his birthday to October 1st of solar calendar for ease of

People's Republic of China, since his lunar birthday coincided with October 1st on the

birth date is August 21, 1926, according to the lunar calendar. After the founding of the

Zhai Guangming's Autobiography, stored in the Archives Office of CNPC. His

[5] Office of CNPC, the Archives

Supplementary materials from Zhai Guangming, July 21, 1955, stored in [4]

Zhai Guangming Interview. [3]

Zhai's maternal grandfather had his own property, which supported the

house, and Zhai did not leave Yichang until he was seven years old.

The three children lived with their mother in her father's

August 21, 1926.[5]

chang in Wuhan, Hubei Province, and Zhai himself in Yichang, Hubei on

Qing-yun in Jingxian County, Anhui province, the elder brother Zhai Guang-

Zhai and his two siblings were born in different places, the elder sister Zhai

Zhai's grandfather was a minor official in the Qing Dynasty (1644-1911). His parents both grew up in Anhui Province. His father worked for many years in the salt business in Jinshanwei, Shanghai, and rarely went home for family reunions.[3] His mother, Zhai Youqing, was born in 1894.[4] Since his father worked away from home and could not take care of the family, his mother had no choice but to live with her father's family in Yichang, Hubei Province. Sometimes she would also move to the home of other relatives in other places.

Fig. 1-1: *Zhai Clan Genealogy of Shuidong*

[6]-[9] Zhai Guangming Interview.
[10] Zhai Guangming's Autobiography, stored in the Archives Office of CNPC.

his mother caught up with her two brothers over family matters, though the

Wuhan first, staying with his eldest and second uncles for a few days, where

he was full of excitement and curiosity. The family of three took a boat to

In 1932, accompanying his mother to Tianjin was Zhai's first long trip, and

Nanjing before settling in Shanghai later.[10]

school, and after graduating from high school, she stayed briefly in Tianjin and

filled with hope and dreams. His sister, Zhai Qingyun, stayed in Yichang for

embarking on a journey to join their relatives in search of a school education,

his mother took Zhai and his brother, Zhai Guang-chang, away from Yichang,

Thus,

lived in Tianjin and had no son, hoped his family would move to Tianjin.[9]

third paternal aunt and aunt-in-law (the wife of his father's elder brother), who

long time, also felt somewhat uneasy. In addition, Zhai's paternal grandmother,

tuition became a major issue. His mother, having lived at her parents' home for a

growing up at his third uncle's home. Which school to attend and how to raise

As Zhai reached school age later, he first had an idea of going to school while

up through thick and thin.

home, not to mention paternal love, and it was his mother who brought him

father. As a child, Zhai could not receive any education from his father at

with his education and learning, leaving him with vague impression of his

His father's care for him was inconceivable, let alone any help

remember.[8]

little contact with him and seeing him only once or twice as far as he could

between them. Zhai had almost no deep impression of his father, with very

his wife and children in Yichang, and there was little correspondence

In his childhood, Zhai led a very monotonous life. His father rarely visited

and division.

maternal grandparents, uncle and aunt, inevitably leading to some tension

his living standard. It also brought inconvenience to the daily life of his

increased the financial burden on his third uncle and significantly lowered

The addition of Zhai's family of four, however,[7]

family relatively well-off.

Yichang, mainly engaged in business related to electricity, making the

while the third inherited his father's property in[6]

working in Wuhan,

family's livelihood. Zhai had three uncles, the eldest and the second uncles

12 Zhai Guangming Interview.[11]

shops lining the streets and rows of small Western-style buildings standing

a scene of prosperity, with merchants gathering from all over the world,

services, mining, modern education and judiciary. In the 1930s, Tianjin was

and pioneered the development of railways, telegraphs, telephones, postal

countries and regions. It opened the door to China's military modernization,

(1861-1895) in modern China, with concessions established by multiple

was also the most open city and the base for the Westernization Movement

in China and the largest financial and commercial center in the north. It

Tianjin at that time was the second largest industrial and commercial city

full of hope and longing for the future.

thinking that she would soon see her relatives, her heart no longer heavy, but

His mother would look at her two young boys, a smile appearing on her face,

in one carriage, it would be full of laughter and joy, chattering and shouting.

the floor against their luggage in the aisles. When there were a few children

finding everything fresh. The carriages were full of people, and some sat on that, occasionally leaning out of the window to see the scenery outside, would run around in the swaying carriages, excitedly looking this way and groceries, making the platform very lively. During the train journey, Zhai north. There were also people seeing off or picking up passengers, or selling for business, for education, or for dreams, coming and going from south to in long robes and jackets, were busy with their own affairs, for livelihood, and off. Passengers from all walks of life, with backpacks and umbrellas, stopped, Zhai would run onto the platform to watch passengers getting on bridges. Along the way, the train stopped at every station, and whenever it sounding its long whistle as it whizzed through jungles, villages, fields, and like an iron ox with immense power. The locomotive panted heavily, traveled far. Zhai had never seen such a big creature running on rails before, a train was quite novel for a child from an ordinary family who had never From Yichang, via Wuhan and Nanjing, they went north to Tianjin. Taking the family's journey north to Tianjin by train.

It was the first time he had been to Nanjing, which was the starting point of

downtown and rich cultural atmosphere left a favorable impression on him.

got a taste of the metropolis, the ancient capital of six dynasties. Its bustling

where they stayed at the home of his second paternal aunt. It was there Zhai

Then, they took a boat from Wuhan to Nanjing,

time for reunion was short.[11]

that has influenced his entire life.

of confidence and hope for life, it is this tenacity and integrity of his mother

to endure hardships without complaining and with perseverance, always full

him and his siblings. Daring to face adversity and fight against fate, willing

exerting a significant impact on

heavy burden of the family on her own,[14]

Zhai's mother, literate, gentle, and virtuous, worked very hard to carry the

delicacy and barrier when living in someone else's home," Zhai recalled.[13]

that time, but it left a lasting impression on me that there was always some

inevitably occurred over time. "I don't remember clearly what's happened at

in-law. As they struggled to make ends meet, some unpleasant incidents

and cooking, weaving and mending clothes, and taking care of her mother-

mother, who was unemployed, took on all the household chores, washing

---

[12]-[14] Zhai Guangming Interview.

When the four members of the Zhai family joined this large family, his

passed away, and then moved to Nanjing.[12]

and she was very kind and filial to her mother. She took care of her until she

on a tight budget. His aunt had been widowed early and never remarried,

Zhai's paternal aunt was a nurse, and only with her income, the family lived

they moved to Tianjin, his sister Zhai Qingyun also came to join them.

his grandmother, aunts and an elder female cousin. The following year after

were making a living elsewhere and only women remained at home, including

Zhai and his elder brother, added joy to them, since all the men of the family

The grandmother had a large family in Tianjin. The arrival of the two boys,

arrived at his grandmother's house in Tianjin.

there were. Full of questions and confusion, yet hopeful, Zhai and his family

was inspired, wondering how big the world was and how many novel things

had never been seen in the small city of Yichang. Watching all these, Zhai

and shops were brightly lit, presenting a sight of peace and prosperity that

rickshaws. At night, the street lamps emitted a yellow glow, and the stores on both sides. The streets were bustling with people, cars, bicycles, and

Chapter 2
Tireless Learning Despite Difficulties

15 (photo courtesy of Zhai Guangming) Tianjin, 1938

Zhai's elementary school photo in Fig. 2-1

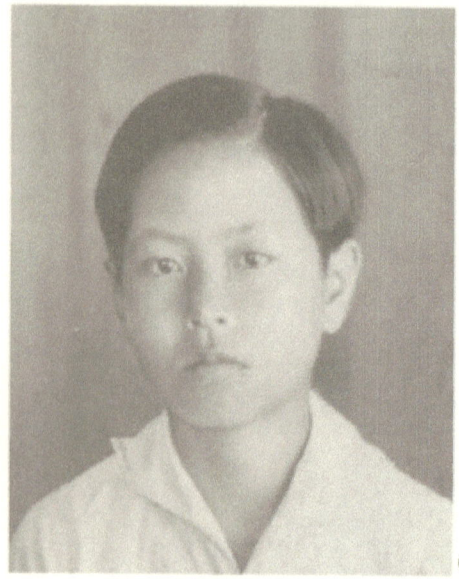

Collecting Project Database.

Zhai Guangming Interview, September 17, 2013, Beijing: Materials stored in the

[1]_____ with the concept shifting from

changed to modern education, methods of teaching gradually

Accordingly, the content and up various types of schools.

quality of its citizens, setting more attention to improving the

During that period, China paid years and two senior years.

year program, with four junior schools in Tianjin adopted a six-

2.1 Tianjin Huiwen Elementary School

When they stayed at the grandmother's house in Tianjin, Zhai Guangming's father had little contact with them. Zhai and his brother, the only two young men in the family, reached school age very soon, as did his cousin. This left the family in a quandary, as they were struggling to feed and clothe themselves, and having to raise the considerable tuition fees was like adding frost to the snow. Despite the difficulties, the family was still very supportive of the education of the three children, doing everything they could to raise the money. Through their great efforts, Zhai was able to enroll at Tianjin Huiwen Elementary School, a private school.[1] Thanks to his mother's asking for a favor and his aunt's personal connections, the school waived part of his tuition. Even so, the burden on the family was still heavy, and they gritted their teeth to get through it. At that time, primary

a nurse at Peking Union Medical College Hospital with very low salary.[6]

To

earn more money and take better care of her mother, she resigned from her

formal position at the hospital and returned to her mother's home in Tianjin

to work as a full-time private nurse for the Lu family. Not only did she earn

a much higher salary than she did at the hospital, but she could also improve

Zhai Guangming Interview, September 17, 2013. [2]

Mr. Lu Muzhai: His Life and Wang Weizhong & Wang Yanqi, [3]

[4] 2012, internal materials, Tianjin No. 24 Middle School. Deeds, September 18,

Lu Muzhai (1856-1948), first name Jing, style name: Mianzhi, and artistic name:

Zhiye Laoren in his later years, a native of Xiantao Town, Mianyang City (now called

Xiantao), Hubei Province. He was a modern book collector and engraver, educator, and

[5] industrialist.

Muzhai Middle School and Me, September 10, 2012, Wang Weizhong & Wang Yangi,

internal materials, Tianjin No. 24 Middle School.

16 Zhai Guangming Interview, September 17, 2013. [6]

education, and from pure elite education to an emphasis on education for the common people. Against this backdrop, Zhai studied at Huiwen Elementary School for six years and got through it smoothly.

2.2 Tianjin Muzhai Middle School

In 1939, after graduating from the elementary school, Zhai attended Tianjin Muzhai Middle School.[2] The middle school was a private one[3] founded in 1932 by the famous educator Mr. Lu Mu-zhai[4], at what is now No. 1 Minquan Road, Jianguo Avenue, Hebei District, Tianjin. To commemorate the founder, a white marble statue of Mr. Lu stands in the teaching building of the school campus today. Since its establishment, the Muzhai Middle School had always adhered to its motto of "sincerity, simplicity, diligence and courage"[5] proposed by Mr. Lu, and maintained operation with thrifty and economical practices.

Mr. Lu was a great help to Zhai's family. At that time, Zhai's aunt worked as

the technical education and the cultivation of specialists to national quality

171940 (photo courtesy of Zhai Guangming)

Zhai's middle school photo in Tianjin, Fig. 2-2

Zhai Guangming Interview, September 17, 2013. [8] evolved from Shandong pancake.

Gaba, or 'guoba', is a unique snack in Tianjin, Gaba, or 'guoba [7]

plenty of opportunities to practice his English with them, and he developed

Tianjin, many children could speak a few words of English, giving Zhai

and literature. As the Muzhai Middle School was in the concession area of

During his junior high school years, Zhai's favorite subjects were English

gaba and a sesame pancake.[8]

were accustomed to eating gaba (crispy rice),[7]

lunch. At that time, Tianjin people

and

at noon. His classmate came

To solve the problem, Zhai often

for lunch, therefore, meal expense

and the lunch hour was so tight

to school. It took him about an

and he had to pass through those

Zhai's family lived on Hai

Concession Area, near the British,

Station, was situated in the

The Muzhai Middle School,

so Zhai's lunch was a serving of

he always helped Zhai with his

as a reward for the tutoring, from a relatively well-off family,

coached a classmate on his lessons

for lunch became a headache.

that there was no time to go home

hour to walk from home to school

concessions every day on his way

Avenue, far from the school,

French and Japanese Concessions.

Italian Concession of the Tianjin

close to the Tianjin Railway

financial assistance to Zhai's brother, which was undoubtedly a timely help.

requested that the school waive all tuition fees for Zhai and provided some

kindhearted Mr. Lu, upon learning of the hardships faced by Zhai's family,

aunt and Mr. Lu, coupled with his mother seeking help from her friends, the

the family's living conditions. With the special relationship between his

[9]-[11] Zhai Guangming Interview, September 17, 2013.
[12] Zhai Guangming Interview, March 21, 2014, Beijing: Store location same as Note No.1.
[13] Supplementary materials from Zhai Guangming, July 21, 1955, stored in the Archives Office of CNPC.

18

inconsolable as he would never have a chance to see his brother again.

Guangming lost his only brother, and upon hearing the terrible news, he was

Zhai

Zhai Guang-chang, his wife Wang Juru, and their two young sons.[13]

unexpectedly. On July 28, 1976, an earthquake occurred in Tangshan, killing

However, disaster struck

to some extent and reduced the living burden.[12]

Although the salary was relatively low, it did increase the family's income

transferred to work in labor and wage management at the Tangshan coalfield.

regret. His work at the factory was tough, and not very satisfactory. Later, he

high school, ultimately missing out on university and carrying this lifelong

start working at a wood factory in Tangshan, Hebei, after graduating from

conditions, it was hard to afford the university tuition. With regret, he had to

However, due to the poor family circumstances and difficult living

and Mr. Lu had also offered to sponsor him with his education.

college,[11]

living. Originally, after graduating from high school, he could have gone to

the heavy pressure for the family and solving the difficult problem of

were not much, they could offset a small part of the tuition, partly relieving

which resulted in a partial waiver of his tuition. Although the scholarships

performance was so outstanding that he won scholarships multiple times,

in junior or senior high school could receive scholarships. His academic

requirements. Its students with comprehensive rankings of the top three

of God Mission Bethel School in Tianjin, a private school with very strict

Zhai Guang-chang, Zhai's elder brother, attended the American Assembly

[10] against the bitter fate and difficult life, and to live on bravely.

musicians, which exerted a great influence on him and inspired him to fight

And he listened to the works of Beethoven and other [9]

Jean-Christophe, Call to Arms, and Romain Rolland's *Autumn*, Lu Xun's and *Spring Family*,

favorite literary classics, both Chinese and foreign, such as Ba Jin's

laying a solid foundation in English. At that period, he also read some

tried translating some simple English classic quotes, novels and essays,

middle school years, Zhai ran an English blackboard newspaper, and

Zhai was very attentive every time he attended her classes. During his

teacher, who taught very well and was popular with all the students. And

a particular fondness for English. Moreover, Zhai met an excellent English

Fig. 2-4 Zhai revisits Tianjin Muzhai Middle School on June 19, 2014 (R-L: Shao Yuan-jin, Shi Qing-bao, Zhai Guangming, Wang Yan-qi, Yang Xian-yi, Yan Jianwen, and Cui 19 Jian-dong. Photo credit: Tianjin Muzhai Middle School)

on June 19, 2014 (Photo by Yan Jianwen)

Fig. 2-3 Zhai pays tribute to the statue of Lu Mu-zhai at Tianjin Muzhai Middle School

20 Zhai Guangming Interview, September 17, 2013. [15]

Tianjin. Materials stored in the Collecting Project Database.

Guangming interview record at Tianjin Muzhai Middle School, June 19, 2014, Zhai

[14] _____

him, so where to go became a real big issue for his family. Going back to

his grandmother nor his aunt, and not even his mother could decide for

a clear path? There were no answers, nor could any be found. Neither

Who to talk to? Who could give him some advice? Who could show him

with ambivalence, which kept him awake at night, unable to eat or drink.

to continue living in Tianjin or to find a way out elsewhere. He was torn

family by joining the workforce or to continue his education, whether

with some weight on his mind, wondering whether to support the

graduated from junior high. He also began to have his own consideration,

pressure of living became almost unbearable. In the same year, Zhai

still had to shoulder the heavy burden of household chores. The mounting

for years, was getting weaker and weaker, and was often sick, yet she

His mother, who had been overworking

to Beiping with her daughter.[15]

where she worked, got married and had children. His aunt-in-law moved

family tension and burden, Zhai's sister had gone to Nanjing alone,

own destiny and future. Two years earlier, to make a living and reduce

increased, coupled with social turmoil, everyone began to consider their

and making their life even harder. Friction among family members

In 1942, Zhai's aunt lost her job, cutting off the family's source of income

2.3 Beiping No. 1 High School

attend this school! Thank you, Mr. Lu Mu-zhai; thank you, my school!"[14]

years, he was overwhelmed with emotion. "It's really not easy for me to

to the middle school, his alma mater, after an absence of more than seventy

endure hardships and cherish life. On June 19, 2014, when Zhai returned

he was a teenager, he had learned how to be firm in his goals and how to

groundwork for Zhai's later development and influenced his entire life. Since

The learning experience at the Muzhai Middle School built a sturdy

---

[16]-[18] Zhai Guangming Interview, September 17, 2013.

easy for him to achieve such amazing results, mainly due to his hard work

It was not

exceptionally well, with Zhai ranking second of all candidates.[18]

the exam covered math, Chinese, English and history. The results were

continue studying; if not, he would look for a job. The main subjects of

confidence at all, adopting a try-and-see attitude—if he passed, he would

No. 1 High School. There were a lot of candidates, and at first, he had no

with the help of his cousin, Zhai took the entrance exam for the Beiping

so she encouraged him to continue his studies. After arriving in Beiping,

be no great development for him in the future if he started work too early,

workforce, mainly because he was too young, but also because there would

His mother felt sorry for him, and was unwilling to let him join the

streets, strange courtyard ... In short, everything was new.

When Zhai first arrived in Beiping, he had no idea what to expect: strange

helping hand to his family so they could settle down and have a place to stay.

living in two very small rooms. Despite the inconveniences, his cousin lent a

home in his cousin's family. At that time, Zhai's aunt-in-law and cousin were

after, his mother, grandmother and aunt also came to join him and find a

Leaving Tianjin, Zhai went to Beiping alone and settled down. Not long

family.

Telephone Bureau, with a stable income that could barely provide for her

had a job in Beiping, working as a switchboard operator at the Beiping

She was compassionate and did Zhai a great favor. She

finally agreed.[17]

discuss the possibility of moving there. After several talks, his cousin

Zhai contacted his cousin, who had gone to work in Beiping earlier, to

could scrape a living in the imperial city. Once the decision was made,

Leaving Tianjin for Beiping might be a good choice; perhaps they

to go.

period, Zhai's family was really struggling to find a direction or a place

and his income was not high enough to cover their expenses. At that

also seemed unlikely, as his brother had just started working in Tangshan

Returning to Yichang, Wuhan or Nanjing

heard from him ever since.[16]

lost contact during the Japanese invasion of Shanghai, and no one had

Shanghai to look for his father was no longer possible, as his father had

22 Zhai Guangming Interview, September 17, 2013. [20]

Beijing. Materials stored in the Collecting Project Database. 2014, 3,

Guangming interview record at Beijing No. 1 High School, July Zhai [19]

_____ which also had two basketball courts.[20]

footbridge. The teachers' dormitory was in the yard with the playground,

one as the teaching area and the other as the playground, connected by a

Nanluoguxiang (South Gong and Drum Lane), and had two compounds.

The school was located in today's

School, which is still in use today.[19]

Government took over the school and renamed it Beijing No.1 High

(1868-1940) in 1912. On April 1, 1949, the Beijing Municipal People's

the Beiping No.1 Public Middle School by the order of Cai Yuan-pei

Eight Banners Institute of Higher Learning in 1904. It was changed into

Imperial Clan Eight Banners Middle School in 1902, and Imperial Clan

Banners. In 1894, it was built into the Jingzheng Academy, and renamed

Qing Dynasty. It was a school specially set up for the children of the Eight

Banners, was founded in 1644, the first year of the Shunzhi era of the

Beiping No. 1 High School, formerly an official school for the Eight

school in Beiping.

could not afford to lose the opportunity. Thus, in 1942, Zhai entered the high

supportive, saying that they would assist his schooling no matter what, as he

the entrance exam, she was elated, and his cousin's family were also very

or dropping out of school. When his mother learned of her son having passed

meet became a major issue. Zhai was torn between the dilemma of getting in

next problem he had to face was still tuition and meals, and making ends

excitement wore off, there was a slight worry and hesitation, because the

Zhai was overjoyed to finally be able to go to school again. Once the

When he learned the news that he had scored second place in his exams,

enabling him to continue his education.

role in his entrance exams. His cousin's family was a major support to Zhai,

school, which gave him some exposure to English and played an important

had started learning English alphabet and simple words since elementary

at Huiwen Elementary School and Muzhai Middle School in Tianjin. He

The accommodation fee was very low, but each dorm room was small, with eight students living in one. The sanitary conditions were extremely poor, and there was no place to take a bath, so lice and bedbugs often infested the dorm, causing everyone to complain bitterly. His roommates tried every means to eliminate the pests, including fumigation, drowning and burning, but none of these methods could thoroughly solve the issue. They had no choice but to endure it silently, hoping every day that these detestable creatures would disappear from the dorm. That was the first time Zhai had been infected with lice,[21] which left an inerasable shadow in his heart for a lifetime. He was afraid of these small insects, and the very mention of lice would make his skin crawl and him feel itchy terribly. After graduating from university, he was also infested by lice during his fieldwork in the Northwest, eventually reaching a point of fear. After several infestations, he gradually developed a good habit of neatness and hygiene.

---

23 Zhai Guangming Interview, September 17, 2013. [21]

at his cousin's family. Soon afterwards, he moved to the school dormitory.

When Zhai was in high school, he started out living in a cramped little room

Jianwen, Li Fen and Yu Hang. Photo credit: Beijing No.1 High School) Yan

Shi-hong, the fourth from left: Zhai Guangming, starting from the fifth on the left:

Wang Zhai revisits Beijing No.1 High School on July 3, 2014 (the first from left:

Fig. 2-5

[22]-[23] Zhai Guangming Interview, September 17, 2013.
[24] Zhai Guangming Interview, October 17, 2013, Beijing: Materials stored in th Collecting Project Database.
[25] Zhai Guangming Interview, September 17, 2013.

24

The hatred for national and familial enemies was often intertwined with

Japanese invaders occupied Shanghai left his young heart deeply scarred.

The humiliation and the loss of contact with his father after the

streets.[25]

brother when living in Tianjin, as he was beaten by Japanese soldiers on the

family moved to Beiping, Zhai experienced a similar situation with his

he had no way to fight back but to endure and suffer in silence. After the

The young man was indignant at this for his brother, but

his passport.[24]

his brother was once beaten and scolded by them due to a dispute over

soldiers often deliberately made things complicated for the residents, and

the concession, but difficult to get in and out of it every day. The Japanese

mother and himself to look after the old house. It was easy to move into

grandmother, aunt-in-law and brother moved in safely, leaving only his

help of friends, and the family finally moved into the concession area. His

was no exception. With great efforts, they rented a house there with the

the concession area. They tried every means to move in, and Zhai's family

freer and safer than the non-concession area, so everyone wanted to live in

At that time, the concession area was relatively

rigorous body searches.[23]

concession with barbed wire, and anyone entering or leaving had to undergo

measures against the concession area, the Japanese invaders fenced off the

restrict the movement of the residents, yet having no guts to take rash

and drew their curtains tightly, living in fear and not daring to go out. To

Tianjin, and every household on the Taku Road district closed their doors

When Zhai Guangming was 11 years old, the Japanese invaders seized

revealing a kind of youthful resistance.

and his hatred for villains, especially his hatred for the Japanese invaders,

content of his essays vaguely reflected his dissatisfaction with the old society

The teachers often used his essays as model texts for commentary in class.[22]

English and literature, and he was especially good at writing essays. His

his schooling and living. Academically, Zhai's favorite subjects were still

and sent Zhai some money every month, which gave him a huge help for

support the family. Then his sister in Shanghai learned of the situation

brother, who worked in Tangshan, had a very low income and could hardly

to get the money for his living expenses, and who could pay for him? His

During the three years of high school study, the biggest problem was where

with hope, no matter what he did, he always held onto a goal, stuck to his

beliefs. He understood what success and failure were, how to face failure,

how to handle success, and what the eventual outcome would be. Only by

never giving up, not losing heart, daring to fight against fate, did he believe

that tenacity would surely bring rewards.

2.4 Geology Department at Peking University

In August 1945, the Chinese people defeated the Japanese invaders and

achieved a complete victory in the War of Resistance, filling the whole

nation with immense exuberance. At that time, Zhai Guangming, who

was in Beiping, witnessed the festive scenes of the people celebrating the

victory, and personally felt the relief and pride of no longer being bullied

by the Japanese invaders. The pent-up anger buried in his heart was finally

unleashed,[26] and he was genuinely joyous for a long time.

A complete victory in Anti-Japanese War generated the enthusiasm of the

people, especially the young students, who had a patriotic heart to serve the

25 Zhai Guangming Interview, October 17, 2013.[26]

adversity and the will to live through hardship. His heart was always filled against fate and a hard life, and how to survive. He learned perseverance in eternity. However, there was one thing Zhai knew well: how to struggle were very challenging, and life under someone else's roof felt like an significant impact on the rest of his life. The learning and living conditions The difficulties in high school were imprinted in his mind and had a adversities.

resilient, self-reliant and self-supporting, and advancing in the face of forged in him an independent character that is clear-cut in love and hatred, fighting against the old society, poverty, and the Japanese invaders. This has a strong sense of motivation and denunciation, revealing his awareness of the harsh reality of the country. No wonder Zhai's essays were filled with

26 Zhai Guangming Interview, September 17, 2013.[28]

Zhai Guangming Interview, October 17, 2013.[27]

is just like that, describing a person who appears strong but is actually

is all show on the outside but a mess on the inside? An embroidered pillow

PILLOW.[28]When he saw this topic, his eyes lit up: Doesn't it mean that it

The essay topic of the foreign language exam was: EMBROIEDRED

better for him to learn more about physics and chemistry.

College of Science and Engineering because he believed it would be

preferred literature, he applied for the Department of Chemistry in the

unaffordable for ordinary families. In choosing a major, although he

their foreign language proficiency, but the tuition fee was very high,

university. FJCU was very strict with its candidates, emphasizing

results earlier, so that he could test his own ability. As a church-founded

University, so there was no time conflict, and he could find out the

The test date of this university was earlier than that of Peking

FJCU.[27]

and-see attitude and the intention of experiencing it, he first applied for
schedule and content varied from one university to another. With a try-
university entrance exam was not a national standardized test, and the
expenses? Zhai knew very little about these questions. At that time, the
it? What was the admission ratio? What were the tuition fees and living
What was covered in it? What was its scope? How many people took
What did the university entrance exam look like? How was it conducted?
fierce competition.

course, the threshold for their admission was also very high, with extremely
most attractive ones were Peking University and Tsinghua University, but, of
Catholic University (FJCU) by the Holy See. Among these universities, the
Yenching University run by the American Chrisitan Churches and Fu Jen
Beijing Hongda College, among others; and the church-run universities were
University, Republic University of Beiping, Confucian University, and
Chaoyang University, University of China, Sino-French University, Beiping
University, and Beijing Normal University; the private universities were

them, the national universities included Peking University, Tsinghua Beiping, including national, private and church-run universities. Among which one to choose. At that time, there were a variety of universities in applied for university with a sincere heart, wrestling with a decision about country through business or science and technology. In that context, Zhai

---

[29]-[31] Zhai Guangming Interview, September 17, 2013.
[32] Zhai Guangming Interview, October 17, 2013.

department established in China's higher education. As early as 1898, when

The Geology Department of Peking University is the earliest geology

and sister said they would support him no matter what.

brother and sister. His mother was thrilled to hear the news, and his brother

which also eased the worries of his

became a student at Peking University,[32]

of his admission as he had always wanted. In the fall of 1945, Zhai officially

would be able to make it, the family was very surprised and happy to learn

never was a college student in his family and they had never thought that he

Zhai was fortunate enough to be admitted to Peking University. Since there

would be easier to find a job and he could also serve the nation. In the end,

like coal ore, iron ore and gold ore. He envisioned that after graduation, it

doing geological work meant going outdoors to search for minerals,[31]

or familiar at that time. He did not know anything about geology, only that

exam, he applied for the Geology Department, which was not very popular

ensure his admission to the university and to reduce the risk of failing the

Considering the large number of applicants and the intense competition, to

Zhai's performance in mathematics, physics and chemistry was average.

was able to solve his daily life problems with the financial aid. However,

Peking University and the competition was very fierce. Once admitted, he

When Zhai graduated from high school, there were many applicants for

was destined to embark on his lifelong career in petroleum exploration.

where there was a campus he longed for and teachers he admired, where he

up FJCU and applied for the Geology Department of Peking University,[130]

after enrollment. Therefore, the young man, with a patriotic aspiration, gave

attractive about the university was the possibility of receiving student grant

to attend Peking University, the best one in his mind, and what was most

to be admitted to a university. To realize his most sincere wish, he wanted

knowledge level and boosted his self-confidence, as he had never expected

received an admission notice from FJCU. The entrance exam testified his

exam, and his overall scores were also very impressive. Consequently, Zhai

thinking that enabled him to achieve excellent scores in foreign language

It was his solid foundation in foreign language and meticulous logical

pen.[29]

of this, he had a clear idea, and a well-reasoned essay came out from his

weak, caring only about appearance but not inner quality. When he thought

28 *Chinese Geological Education*, 2009 (3), p. 167.

Celebrating the 100th Anniversary of the Geology Department of Peking University.

Pan Mao & Song Zhenqing. One Hundred Years of Striving, Recreating Brilliance:

[35] stratigrapher. and

Amadeus W. Grabau (1870-1946), a German-American geologist, paleontologist,

[34] Beijing: Petroleum Industry Press, 1992. *Foreign Countries.* and China

History of Geological Science Exchange between Wang Hongzhen, [33]

---

accelerating his growth and propelled him into a career of geological oil

system of knowledge. The guidance of eminent teachers acted like a catalyst,

his knowledge base, stimulating his mind and continually enriching his

tectonics, petrology, mineral deposits ... A vast array of new terms entered

opening experience for Zhai. Trilobites, mineral crystals, fossils, strata,

Entering the Geology Departmen at the College of Science was an eye-

outstanding geologists who graduated from the department.

Zhai is one of the

can be honored as "the cradle of Chinese geologists".[35]

trained a great pool of outstanding geological personnel for the country, and

institution in China, the Geology Department of Peking University has

geological talents of higher learning and the earliest geological academic

Brown Barbour, and Peter Misch. As the first teaching institution to cultivate

Friedrich Solger, G. A. Adams, Aysal, George

Amadeus William Grabau,[34]

yuan, Li Chun-yu, and Wang Zhu-quan. The foreign professors included

Xi-chou, Yuan Fu-li, Yang Zhong-jian, Hou Ren-zhi, Le Sen-xun, Ma Xing-

geologists like Ding Wen-jiang, Zhang Hong-zhao, Weng Wen-hao, Tan

Xie Jia-rong, and Sun Yun-zhu, among others. Its faculty consisted of many

of the Department were He Jie, Wang Lie, Wang Shao-ying, Li Si-guang,

People's Republic of China in 1949, the scholars who served as the dean

From its establishment to the founding of

tectonics and seismic geology.[33]

gradually expanded to include geochemistry, paleontology and stratigraphy,

Imperial University of Peking, the predecessor of Peking University, was founded, there was a plan to establish a geology discipline. In 1909, the university began to set up disciplines of chemistry and geology, which were suspended due to financial constraints. In 1916 the Geology Discipline was reopened and resumed its enrollment in 1917, with two subjects, namely, paleontology and economic geology. In 1923, a subject of mineralogy and petrology was added. During the Anti-Japanese War, the Geology Department moved south with Peking University to Changsha, Kunming and other cities, during which time specialties of geology, geography and meteorology were added. After several changes, the Department was

29 stored in the Archives Office of CNPC. years,

Zhai Guangming's transcript at Peking University over the four academic

[36]　　　　　　　Wei-zhou.

crystallography from Mr. Yu Rui-huang, and mineral deposits from Mr. Ruan

paleobotany from Mr. Si Xing-jian, geophysics from Mr. Gu Gong-xu, X-ray

Ji-qing, paleontology from Mr. Sun Yun-zhu and Mr. Wang Hong-zhen,

He learned tectonics from Mr. Huang

and Geophysical Prospecting.[36]

Experiment, Tectonics and Experiment, Mineral Deposits and Experiment,

Zoology and Experiment, Paleontology and Experiment, Physiography and

General Botany and Experiment, Petrology and Experiment, General

Optical Mineralogy and Experiment, Topography and Experiment,

Geology, General Mineralogy and Experiment, Geology and Experiment,

courses mainly consist of Qualitative Analysis and Experiment, General

Mr. Sun Cheng'e, and German with Mr. Wei De-ming. The specialized

general chemistry with Mr. Zhang Long-xiang, physical chemistry with

physics with Mr. Zheng Hua-chi, electrical knowledge with Mr. Ma Da-you, and Organic Chemistry. During his time at university, Zhai studied general History of China, Chinese Language, English, Political Science, German, or gaseous mineral deposits. The basic courses mainly include General or metallic mineral deposits, with almost no courses related to liquid ones. In terms of the overall curriculum design, the emphasis is on solid required and elective courses, which are divided into basic and specialized can see the full picture of the university curriculum at that time, including academic year with an average score of 70.5. From the transcript, you with an average score of 69.92; and there were 4 courses in the fourth an average score of 68.9; there were 9 courses in the third academic year score of 71.5; in the second academic year, there were 12 courses with and 1949. In the first academic year, there were 7 courses with an average university shows his grades of four academic years: 1945, 1947, 1948 exploration was the focus in the early days. The transcript of Zhai at the

Since its establishment, the teaching of general geology and solid mineral exploration.

30 Zhai Guangming Interview, October 17, 2013.[37]

beneficial throughout his life. One of the most influential teachers on Zhai

gave him a new insight into life, work, study and social skills, which were

Mr. Dong Shen-bao's down-to-earth spirit and Mr. Ma Xing-yuan's vivacity

period, several activists of Peking University also deeply influenced him.

profound impression on Zhai, with far-reaching influence. During that

The lecturers of the specialized courses during his college years left a

engagement in geological research.

new understanding of geology and laid a certain foundation for his future

Through systematic study of basic and specialized courses, Zhai gained a

class periods.[37]

his knowledge of oil and gas was very limited, only a meager two or three

exploitation geology in petroleum exploration & development. Accordingly,

to petroleum geology, let alone the drilling geology, logging geology and

with very few mining-related subjects. There were almost no courses related

During his college years, Zhai mainly studied the basic geological courses,

Zhai Guangming's transcript at Peking University Fig. 2-6

[3] Zhai Guangming Interview, October 17, 2013. [40]

of Geology and the Deputy Director of the Chinese Academy of Geological Sciences.

and stratigraphy. He served as the Director of the Education Department of the Ministry

geologist, and educator, was one of the pioneers and founders of Chinese paleontology

Yunzhu (1895-1979), style name Tie Xian, a famous Chinese paleontologist, Sun

[39] geochemistry.

and Peking University. He was mainly engaged in research and teaching in petrology and

geologist at the United States Geological Survey, and a professor at Beiyang University

at Peking University in 1935, served as a geologist at the Central Geological Survey, a

Geology Department Ruan Weizhou (1912-1998), geologist, graduated from the

[38] _____

to the lectures of renowned teachers, studied rock specimens, and explored

years in such a mysterious palace of geology. In this museum, they listened

rock slices together. Zhai Guangming and his classmates spent their college

attended classes, conducted experiments, observed rock specimens and made

where his classmates and him

Geological Museum of Peking University,[40]

During his college years, Zhai's main activities were centered around the

students and benefited Zhai greatly as well.

earnest practice and sincere teachings have influenced the lives of their

who have played a vital role in Zhai's cultivation and education, and whose

various setbacks and failures." It was these teachers, like Professor Sun,

every scientific and technological worker to be strong and able to withstand

like other professions, can teach us many life philosophies. It requires

conditions, I have always believed that work in science and technology,

no matter in the success or failure, in difficult environments or favorable

become a scientific and technological worker. In the ensuing long career,

technology, and the years of field geological surveys have trained me to

of the day. My college education has brought me to the door of science and

"Any success comes from endless effort, just as the night is the affirmation

had been taught by him would cherish his words forever. Sun once said,

his studies, and rewarded and promoted his students. All the students who

Department at Peking University. He was rigorous, sincere and earnest in

talents in China and to the construction and development of the Geology

college. Sun made an indelible contribution to the cultivation of geological

was the dean of the Geology Department when Zhai was in

Sun Yun-zhu[39]

Zhai traveled to Taiwan for academic exchanges and met with Ruan,

dean of the Geology Department of National Taiwan University. Years later,

was Professor Ruan Wei-zhou[38], who later went to Taiwan and served as the

was Professor Ruan Wei-zhou[38]

32 *Scientific Chinese*, 2003 (6), pp. 52-53. Peking University.

Weixing. Chronicles of the Geology Department (Hall) at Hu [44]

Collecting Project Database.

Interview, November 6, 2013, Beijing: Materials stored in the Zhai Guangming

[43] Geosciences, at China University of

University in 1950. He is an academician of the CAS and a professor

educator. Born in Shanghai in 1924, he graduated from the Geology Department at Peking

geological Yu Chongwen, a geochemical dynamicist, mineral deposit geochemist, and

[42] and a well-known hydrogeologist.

University in 1951 as a graduate student, researcher at the Xinjiang Branch of the CAS,

Liang Kuangyi (1927-2014), graduated from the Geology Department at Peking

[41] _____

The Geological Museum was formerly the showroom of the Geology

actions of the KMT military police.[44]

protecting the school and teachers and students, effectively preventing the

police stormed the university to arrest students, they were the main force in weapons. In several incidents in which the Kuomintang (KMT) military at night, with geology hammers as their most traditional and most practical the west gate of the university, there they were, standing guard or patrolling defense team. Whether in the Xizhai dormitory near the Jingshan Street, or at more so in the defense of the school, for many of them joined in the school main force of the student picket teams in all student movements, and even to respond, ready to fight, and sure to win". Therefore, they were always the fitness, organization and discipline, they gained the reputation of "prompt action. Moreover, as the students of the Department were generally better in various activities they showed great unity and a high degree of unison in special academic environment and unique way of learning and lifestyle. In of the Geology Department were famous in Peking University for their

The teachers and students

acted in unison, going together or not at all.[43]

and Wang Shen-quan. No matter what activities they participated in, they

Xu Wang, Jin Kui-li, Zhang Peng-fei, Gao Shu-ping, Li Ze-xin, Huang Qiao,

Hu Wei-xing, Yu Chong-wen,[42]

with his classmates like Liang Kuang-yi,[41]

and formed profound bonds of affection. Zhai spent his college years here

particularly deep and close. They cared for each other, helped each other,

emotional ties among classmates, and between teachers and students were

The Geological Museum was a small independent world, where the

strength for prospecting and mining in their future career.

the mysteries of the earth to enrich their knowledge and accumulate their

33 the unit being yuan.

ROC. In the 23rd year of the ROC, i. e., 1934, the legal currency was silver coins, with

National Currency Regulations, establishing silver dollars as the national currency of the

In 1914, the Nanjing government of the Republic of China (ROC) introduced the

[45]

southern part has three stories, and the north part has two stories except

The museum is "L-shaped, covering an area of 791 square meters. The

Professors Li Si-guang and Ding Wen-jiang of the Geology Department."

regular expenses of the university, and will be supported by donations from

covered by the special fund set up by the university and the CFPEC and the

The fees will be

than 5,500 yuan, it amounted to more than 66,000 yuan.[45]

engineer design fees. Together with the cost of other equipment of more

yuan for civil engineering, heating and sanitation, electrical engineering and

of China, completed in July the next year, with a total coast of over 60,000

construction of the museum "started in May, the 23rd year of the Republic

commemorate his merit in the expedition to Jinchuan. It is recorded that the

courtyard stands a stele erected by the imperial command of Qianlong to

in the reign of Emperor Qianlong (1736-1795) of the Qing Dynasty. In the

temple, which was originally the home temple of the grand scholar Fu Heng

is also known as the Song Gong ancestral *Shatan Beijie*

15 courtyard near *Songgongfu*, improving the school conditions. The No.

student dormitory at

were used to build new facilities such as library, geological museum and

special fund for cooperative research was established. Some of the funds

for the Promotion of Education and Culture (CFPEC) was secured and a

with the efforts of Hu Shih and others, funding from the China Foundation

Republic of China. In December 1930, after Jiang assumed the presidency,

Meng-lin, President of Peking University, on May 15, the 23rd year of the

is engraved with the following words: The cornerstone was laid by Jiang

embedded in the wall below the southwest corner of the building, which

in the history of Chinese modern architecture. There is a cornerstone

western modernist architecture in China and holds an important position

and Lin Hui-yin, which is an excellent work of the earliest introduction of

of the works designed by the famous Chinese architects Liang Si-cheng

history of Chinese architecture and the geological development. It is one

shape, function and collections, it has secured a memorable place in the

functional requirements. Speaking of the museum, from its construction,

asymmetrical plan and elevation, and its shape varies according to the

North Street), housed in a gray Western-style three-story building with

(Beach *Shatan Beijie*

Department. It is in the No. 15 courtyard, west of the

34

far as Jiapigou gold mine in Jilin, Kailuan coal mine in Tangshan, Hebei, locations for fieldtrip were important mining areas in China at that time, as Geological fieldtrip is an important activity of the university. The main for students.

objects recording the history of the earth open the door to the natural world teaching and experiments. The abundant variety of earth minerals and over the world are gathered here, providing a base for geological research, of geological teaching specimens and typical geological specimens from all identified, and mineral crystals show the shape of each system. The essence with corresponding slices, while minerals and fossils have been accurately paleontological fossil specimens, with each set of rock specimens equipped systematic and complete sets of rocks, minerals, mineral crystals and dolomite clusters, realgar single crystals and other treasures. It also possesses tortoises, crystal pyrite clusters, orpiment calcite clusters, stibnite clusters, museum has grown increasingly abundant, including trilobites, Maoming

exploration and international geological exchanges, the collection of the set up. With the continuous deepening and broadening of domestic mineral Paleobotany Exhibition Room and Mineral Rock Exhibition Room were Geology Exhibition Room, Paleontology and Stratigraphy Exhibition Room. After the completion of the Geological Museum in 1935, the Dynamic specimens of paleontology, minerals, rocks, and geological structures. As early as 1917, the Geological Showroom had displayed more than 1,000 building in Peking University.

the science departments to have an independent teaching and experimental of Peking was situated, to the Geological Museum, becoming the first one of building for the College of Science), where the former Imperial University was moved from the North Building of the Second Compound (teaching display, and faculty room." In August 1935, the Geology Department rock display, and faculty room; and the third floor as classroom, geological laboratory, microphotographic room, mineral deposit practice room, mineral faculty room, and staff studio; the second floor as classroom, auditorium, geohistorical display, darkroom, reading room, student research room,

room, and boiler room; the first floor as classroom, paleontology display,

Beijing." Inside the museum, "the cellar is used as grinding room, storage

by Liang Si-cheng, and contracted by Weihua and Haijing factories in

are made of reinforced concrete, while the rest is made of bricks, designed

for the cellar. The floor of the roof and the main load-bearing members

35 Xie Hongyuan, et al., 2000.[49](4), p. 298.

Journal of University of Science and Technology Anshan, Aug. 2004

Mining Technology.

Lu Weiping. Geology of Gold Ore in Jiapigou Valley and Brief History of Its

[48] Jan. 2000 (1), p. 111. *Chinese Journal of Geology*,

Geological Problems of Jiapigou Gold Belt, Jilin Province.

Yuanchao & Jiao Xudong. Discussion on Some Important Xie Hongyuan & Shen

[47] Zhai Guangming Interview, November 6, 2013. [46] _____

porphyrite, granodiorite and so on.[49]

isotopic chronology data. The main vein rocks are syenite porphyry, diorite

in the early Precambrian and Hercynian-Indosinian periods according to

granitic rocks are widely distributed within the region, mainly concentrated

of the tectonic belt is the dumbbell-shaped Proterozoic potassic granite. The

the Anshan Group of Archean hornfels-granulite facies, while the lower part

granite-greenstone belt, mainly exposing the metamorphic rock complex of

west tectonic belt of Jiapigou, the eastern part of the zone is the Jiapigou

plate and the southern edge of the Jiamusi block. Bounded by the north-

between the eastern part of the northern edge of the Sino-Korean paleo-

quartz veins, and the gold metallogenic belt is located near the contact zone

The ore type of Jiapigou is mainly alloy minerals in

resumed in 1946.[48]

Japanese War, it returned to the people's embrace, and the production was

was occupied by the Japanese invaders, and after the victory of the Anti-

source of financial revenue for the region. In the early years, the gold mine

of China's non-ferrous metal industry; and gold mining was an important

China, was a very famous gold mine in the country, once called the cradle

North Korea. The town of Jiapigou, known as the premier gold town in

and Korean ethnic group, and close to the borderline between China and

beautiful scenery and rich wildlife resources. It is inhabited by Han people

upper reaches of the Songhua River. Surrounded by mountains, it boasts

southeastern Jilin Province, at the foot of the Changbai Mountains and the

Huadian County,

gold mine in Jilin. The goldmine is in Jiapigou Town,[47]

As Zhai recalls, he was most impressed by his internship at the Jiapigou cradle for training geological workers.

1949, and served as a field laboratory for geology. And Xishan became the Zhoukoudian base for geological teaching and practice was built before The

and as close as Mentougou, Zhoukoudian, and Xishan in Beijing.[46]

[50]-[51] Zhai Guangming Interview, October 17, 2013.
[52] Lu Weiping, 2004, p. 300.

36

there was once a geological internship at Kailuan coal mine in Tangshan. According to the recollection of Hu Wei-xing, Zhai's university classmate, mine after graduation.

determination to find and develop minerals, and longed for a job in a metal research on mineral deposits and the lack of talents, which strengthened his of the country's mineral species, and saw the weakness of its geological conditions of the local residents. He also became aware of the richness of miners, and learned about the mining process and the difficult living During his geological internship at Jiapigou, Zhai witnessed the hard labor was used for gold extraction, but the environment was badly damaged. water, which is often referred to as "panning for gold". Later, amalgamation cracked, and then it was crushed by a stone roller, and finally panned in and water agitation method was used to make the ore become quenching

After the ore was mined, the fire

shaped coring" techniques were adopted.[52]

improvement, "cone-shaped coring", "wedge-shaped coring" and "drug pot-

of gold mining was to use spade and pickaxe to extract gold ore, and after

The most primitive method

pollution; and the miners suffered even more.[51]

of mining. Moreover, the mining process was outdated, causing excessive

behind all lean ore and tailings, which posed great difficulties for restoration

predatory and destructive mining in the hands of Japanese invaders, leaving

or trek, to be more precise. The Jiapigou gold ore had suffered years of

dozens of kilometers, all mountain roads, making it very difficult to travel,

to the district of Laoniugou. The distance between the mining fields was

process; most of them were in the Jiapigou mining lot, while one group went

went to different mining areas to observe outcrops and the gold mining

The teams

were divided into several teams, with Zhai in a team of four.[50]

Nevertheless, the miners did their best to entertain the college students, who

dining tables; and the rooms in which they were staying looked shabby.

It happened to be summer and flies were prevalent in the kitchen and on

had resumed production, the living and sanitary conditions were terrible.

internships amidst chaos of war. Since it was not long after the gold mine

were also curious and surprised: it was not easy for students to come for

to it and treated the students and teachers as honored guests. The miners

went to a remote gold mine. The person in charge attached great importance

During the geological internship of that year, students of Peking University

37 Hu Weixing, 2003. [53] _____

delighted and wished they would meet the PLA right away.

Seeing that liberation was imminent, every teacher and student was truly

terrified, each one like a bird frightened by the mere twang of a bowstring.

the PLA was getting very close. At that moment, the KMT defenders were

Another gain of this internship was that they got an important message that

brought back to the Geological Museum and became part of its collection.

trilobite fossil, which was extremely precious. These specimens were later

days was very fruitful. Fortunately, one student even collected a large

lithology and draw geological profiles. The internship over those several

various geological outcrops and lithology, collect rock specimens, record

was very limited. Even so, the students still went up the hilltop to observe

be shot right away. As a result, the range available for internship observation

to enter the restricted area or cross the blockade line, otherwise they would

Although they were allowed to go, the KMT soldiers still warned them not

misunderstanding was cleared up and they were allowed to pass through.

their student identity and they were conducting a field practice, that the

was only after patient and detailed explanations, in which they clarified

glasses, and cameras, as if they were soldiers ready to launch an attack. It

with map cases, saddlebags, geological hammers, binoculars, magnifying

mistaken the students for the PLA because the students were fully "armed"

made contact with the armed KMT soldiers, who then realized that they had

on the ground, not daring to raise their heads. After much effort, they finally

overhead, making them so nervous that they alerted each other to lie down

a hilltop, suddenly there was a loud burst of gunfire, and bullets whizzed

and encountered trouble immediately. When they were about to approach

the next day, they went to the Kailuan coal mine for a short field internship,

students stayed in the university dormitory on the first day of their trip. On

self-governing association of Tangshan Jiaotong University, the team of

and the range of activities was greatly restricted. With the help of the student

making it very difficult to carry out field geological surveys in Tangshan,

and dense electric fences. The KMT defenders enforced strict inspection, and Tangshan was like an isolated island, surrounded by numerous bunkers

the People's Liberation Army (PLA) had already entered the Shanhai Pass,

take a train to Kaiping Basin in Tangshan for field practice. At that time,

who had recently returned to China, led a team of teachers and students to

It was in the second half of 1948. Mr. Wang Hong-zhen,

Hebei Province.[53]

[54]-[55] Zhai Guangming Interview, November 6, 2013.

38

extremely weak, and it is contagious. In the end, nobody was willing to care

fever is a severe disease with persistent high fever that leaves people feeling

Zhai contracted black fever, which was like adding insult to injury. Black

mosquitoes and flies. As a result, soon after recovering from the dysentery,

camp had no screens on the windows, there were particularly a lot of

However, misfortunes never come singly. As the houses at the summer

of suffering, he finally pulled through and his health improved day by day.

and relied on his classmate Liang to help him with his meals. After a period

lying alone in the dorm every day, with virtually no one to take care of him,

activities, while Zhai was too sick to get out of bed, unable to do anything,

weeks, putting him in severe trouble. The campers went out for various

the camp, leaving him no choice but to suffer. The illness lasted for several

no effective medicine for dysentery. Unfortunately, there was no doctor in

there was a shortage of doctors and medicine under KMT rule, and there was

At that time, shortly after the victory of Anti-Japanese War, dysentery.[55]

attention to what he ate, coupled with poor sanitary conditions, Zhai caught after joining the camp, something happened. Since he did not pay much room, each with a simple set of luggage and one set of bedding. Not long conditions were very bad, with more than twenty people staying in one After that, they lived a communal life just like in the army. The late.[54]

and added to two teams that had already been allocated because they were Zhai and his classmate Liang Kuang-yi were assigned to the reserve group (YLTPP), but it was not made clear at first. On the first day of registration, organized by the KMT's Youth League of the Three Principles of the People he arrived at the camp, the atmosphere smelled different. The camp was or housing, only playing, and he would be delighted to join it. But once initial imagination of the camp was very tempting, no worries about meal garden tours, mountain climbing, swimming, running, and singing. His

provided food and lodging, as well as activities such as intensive training, for a summer camp. This camp, set up at Wanshou Mountain in Beijing, together a meal and have something to do during the holiday, he signed up scholarships and living expenses, so he had no money for food. To scrape university dining hall and dormitories were closed, and it no longer issued but he ultimately graduated in 1950. In the summer vacation of 1946, the college year. He was supposed to graduate in 1949 after enrolling in 1945, progress was not very smooth. He took a year off due to illness in his second During his college years, Zhai had a really tough time, and his academic

a puncture operation and further tests and treatments, and along with very

[56]-[57] Zhai Guangming Interview, November 6, 2013.

finally identified the disease and found the cause. He promptly performed

and promised to treat Zhai. After careful diagnosis and treatment, the doctor

from the Peking Union Medical College Hospital, who ran a private clinic

search for a doctor. Through their efforts, they finally found a retired doctor

treatment, selling off her belongings and clothes, with his sister joining in the

and watch her child suffer like that, so she went around looking for medical

mother saw it all and felt pain in her heart. She could no longer stand by

effective measure, so he just dragged on, almost to the point of death. His

and was very sick, he was left to fend for himself. His family did not have

guild hall without having to pay rent. When he came down with black fever

because of their hometown connections. In that way, Zhai moved into the

discussions with the person in charge, they finally agreed to lend her a room

contacted the Guild Hall through the help of friends, and after repeated

Hutong near Qianmen, which were temporarily unoccupied. His mother there were several empty rooms in the Jingxian Guild Hall at Xianyukou he had a contagious disease, and physical distancing was necessary. Luckily, Zhai was placed in the other. However, this was not a long-term solution, as house only had two small rooms, with the women crammed into one, and The cousin's
period, his mother, sister, and aunt were also in Beijing.[57]
continue his schooling, so he had to stay at home for recovery. At that Back at his cousin's home, Zhai did not improve much, and he could not recuperate.[56]
Liang had no choice but to escort him to his cousin's house in Beiping to leave immediately. In the end, he was unable to withstand the pressure, and the instructor firmly refused to let Zhai stay any longer, demanding him to little food. In a few days, the camp was in utter chaos like a bombed temple; it out in the camp, refusing to leave, as he could at least scrape together a there was no money to buy them. What could he do? He just had to tough

properly. At that time, there were no medicines, and even if there were,

be overcome on one's own, and it could be life-threatening if not handled

his miserable life. Unlike dysentery, black fever is not a disease that can

no one cared wherever he went. He was at his wits' end, sighing alone over

they wanted to expel Zhai from the camp. He had nowhere else to go, and

the instructors and campers were worried about a widespread outbreak, so

for him. The camp was full of people who were afraid of being infected, and

40 Weixing, 2003. Hu [59] Zhai Guangming Interview, November 6, 2013.

[58] _____

team of the College of Science, and represented it in many basketball

Wangfujing in Beijing. Both of them were selected to join the basketball

playing basketball. He often played it with Zhai at the Christian Church near

excellent, but also very lively, with a wide range of hobbies, especially

Liang was not only academically

achieving numerous results and honors.[59]

dedicating his life to geological and geographical research in West China,

the Xinjiang Institute of Geography of the Chinese Academy of Sciences,

Department of Philosophy at Peking University, and was later assigned to

After graduating from the university, he pursued his graduate studies in the

talent for languages, proficient in English, French, Russian and German.

a variety of activities. Now let us know more about Liang, who had a great

together, studying, playing ball games, attending concerts, and engaging in

help dancing. With his good friend back at last, they started a new life

him back, especially Liang Kuang-yi, who was so happy that he couldn't

vigor, and returned to his classmates. His classmates were excited to see

After recovering from his illness, Zhai was like a changed person, full of

value of trials and tribulations.

and so unpredictable that only by experiencing it can one truly appreciate the

just as the saying goes: Every cloud has a silver lining. Life is so marvelous

later life, and he was not greatly impacted by subsequent movements. This is

summer camp organized by the YLTPP, which saved much trouble in his

a long road ahead. Of course, this illness also kept Zhai away from the

can be acquired again, academic delays can be made up, and there is still

great scientist. As long as there is life, everything can start over. Possessions

valuables. But ultimately, a life was saved, a vibrant life, the life of a future

whatever they could, leaving almost nothing in their life, not to mention

even poorer. To raise money for the treatment, the family sold and pawned

pulled back from the jaws of death. This serious illness made his family

period of his life. He was truly blessed with a great fortune, and had been

escaped danger and had a brush with death, surviving the most dangerous

Under the meticulous care of his mother and sister, Zhai finally

get better.[58]

and their consolation and expectations gave him confidence that he would

more energetic. During that period, his classmates visited him several times,

regained his appetite, could move around on his own, and gradually became

[60]

ensured that the thousand-year-old capital was returned to the people reborn. General Fu Zuo-yi, with his deep understanding of righteousness, heavy gloom in the hearts of Beiping residents, and the ancient city was and shocking the whole world. This peal of spring thunder swept away the over the ancient capital of one thousand years, shaking the entire China exploded like spring thunder in the dead of winter, rumbling and rolling news that the Chinese People's Liberation Army had marched into Beiping On January 31, 1949, Beiping ushered in a historic moment. On that day, the possible.

were all full of infinite expectations, hoping that day would come as soon as They felt a secret thrill that Beiping was going to be liberated, and they teachers welcoming the arrival of liberation and making dumplings together. However, the museum was brightly lit and bustling with students and bleak, and with sporadic gunshots, there was hardly any festive atmosphere.

41 Weixing, 2003. Hu [61] Zhai Guangming Interview, November 6, 2013.

At that time, Beiping was under siege, desolate and

Geological Museum.[61]

his fellow students held a teacher-student New Year's Eve party in the

According to Hu Wei-xing's memories, on New Year's Day in 1949,

experience.

intermingled, becoming unforgettable memories in his life, enriching his life

confusion, yearning, excitement, disappointment, failure and success were

All of these left a deep imprint on Zhai's mind. Pain, joy, pride, sadness,

ceremony of PRC, and experienced upheavals and changes in the old society.

the entry of the PLA into Beijing and the preparatory work for the founding

He also engaged in publicity activities at places like Mentougou, witnessed

hunger, the anti-hunger, anti-corruption and anti-civil war demonstration.

of study and fieldtrip, the torment of illness, the suffering of poverty and

After his admission to Peking University, Zhai went through hardships

predicaments.

and only with a robust physique can one endure the test of various

without a strong body, nearly everything is out of the realm of possibility;

for his future work in petroleum geological exploration. It can be said that

habit that Zhai developed after his illness, laying a solid physical foundation

Loving exercise and sports was a positive

matches with good results.[60]

42 Zhai Guangming Interview, November 6, 2013.[63]

Publishing House, 2012, pp. 357-360. Art

The Old Events of the People of Old Beijing. Beijing: Culture and Mu Gu.[62]

The soldiers were dressed in various kinds of clothes, including captured

tanks, anti-tank guns, anti-aircraft guns, mortars, howitzers, and cannons.

wide variety of weapons and equipment, including trucks, armored vehicles,

vast and powerful, with motorized units, armored units, artillery units, and a

greatly, thinking that the PLA was truly awe-inspiring. The procession was

The marching troops were so majestic and imposing that Zhai admired them

meters west of the Zhengyangmen for several hours.[63]

family were among the crowd welcoming the PLA, and he stood about 200

soldiers in an unprecedented scene of enthusiasm and grandeur. Zhai and his

first light of morning and enthusiastically shook hands and hugged the PLA

welcome, creating a sea of people. The people of Beijing finally saw the

the news and cheering with joy, waving flags and holding up banners of

was no exception. Men and women of all ages took to the streets, spreading

people welcoming the PLA's entry into the city, and the Zhengyangmen

The ceremony lasted from 10 a.m. to 5 p.m. The streets were filled with

yet the procession had not finished until the head and tail were connected.

out of the Hepingmen, while the rear still surging into the Yongdingmen,

Guang'anmen. The marching troops were fully armed, with the leading troop

Chang'an Street, Hepingmen, Mule Market Street, exiting the city through

Taipingcang. After the two troops met, they passed along Xisi, Xidan, West

and then to Chongwenmennei Street, Dongdan, Dongsi, Beixinqiao and

Street and Qianmen Street, through Qianmen to Dongjiaominxiang Alley,

The troops starting from Nanyuan entered the city onto Yongdingmen

split into two routes: one from Xizhimen and the other from Yongdingmen.

the city in formation, presenting a grand scene. The troops entering the city

spring in Beiping, with the cold wind piercing to the bone, the PLA entered

On February 3, the PLA held a formal ceremony to enter the city. In the early

liberated.[162]

did ordinary civilians clearly realize that Beiping had been peacefully PLA soldiers replaced the KMT guards loathed by the common people from Xizhimen to take over the entire defense of Beiping. Only when the Committee, a section of the Fourth Field Army of the PLA entered the city intact. Following the instructions of Chairman Mao Zedong and the Central

[64]-[67] Zhai Guangming Interview, November 6, 2013.

a job in Beijing. What could he do? There was only the option to follow

However, with too few positions available, there was little hope of finding

needed. At first, all the graduates wanted to stay in Beijing, and so did Zhai.

obey the state's assignment and went to the places where they were most

and all the other students would have to

in the Geology Departmen,[67]

posted an announcement that only one teaching assistant would be recruited

primary issue facing every graduate. On the eve of graduation, the university

As the graduation drew near, the question of where to work became the

stabilize. and prices had begun to

the school canteen had also greatly improved,[66]

considerable changes, with better service and food quality. The food of

boiling with exhilaration. And the small restaurants in the city underwent

and energy. The whole university, even the entire city of Beijing, was well-acted." The students were also greatly inspired, each full of enthusiasm "This is the first time I've seen such a performance; it's so beautiful and was deeply touched and burst into tears of fervor. His sister said emotionally, After enjoying the performance, the family

family to watch it together.[65]

the College of Law), Guo Lan-ying performed a drama, and Zhai invited his auditorium of Peking University's Third Compound (a teaching building for including concerts, report meetings, speeches, and debates. In the small back to school, incredibly excited, and then held various celebrations, After watching the PLA march into the city, the teachers and students went but unconsciously followed them for several miles.

like family members, the welcoming crowd was reluctant to part with them,

Watching the various formations of the PLA soldiers,

calmed for a while.[64]

coming, and I will soon live a stable and good life. His ecstasy could not be

weapons himself, so he let go of his voice and cheered: the new life is really proud and excited, but also curious, as if he had captured the enemy's sounds and seeing the weapons and the majestic troops, Zhai felt immensely vehicles and tanks formed a stirring song of triumph. Listening to these clouds. The clip-clop of the horses' hooves and the rumbling of the armored and whistling of the crowd were earth-shattering and echoed through the marching majestically and with a great sense of pride. The singing, cheering most of them wearing gray cotton-padded clothes and carrying duffel bags, American military leather jackets and coarse cotton-padded clothes, with

44 he cherished for a lifetime, and had the fruit of their love.

exploration. It was also there that he met his love, his beloved wife, whom

oil searching, and cultivated his greatest lifelong interest—petroleum

invented the method of fluorescence logging, mastered the real skills of

petroleum knowledge that he had never been exposed to in university,

he met his mentor who guided him on the path of oil exploration, learned

him fall in love with the region and the petroleum industry. It was there that

stayed there for seven years. It was the hardships in the Northwest that made

most. Having made up his mind, Zhai went there without hesitation, and

the Great Northwest, to the place where the motherland needed them the

Republic of China, Zhai's response was to obey the assignment and go to

with a passion and the vigor of youth, and out of his love for the People's

so it seemed he had to start from scratch. After a few days of inner struggle,

in Beijing, for one thing, and he knew nothing about petroleum for another,

To be or not to be? The Northwest was too far away from his so-called home

that the Northwest was the most remote and impoverished place in China.

When he heard the news, his mind went blank at once, and then he realized

was assigned to the newly established Northwest Petroleum Administration.

school were all related to it. However, things did not go as planned, and Zhai

mine, especially a non-ferrous metal mine, because the courses he studied at

the assignment, with the first hope being to be assigned to work in a metal

Chapter 3
Bonding with Oil Exploration in the Northwest

47 manager of the Yanchang Oilfield Exploration Office.

He was a petroleum engineering expert, having previously served as director and mine

Yan Shuang (1896-1962), courtesy name Yingbo, was a native of Taixing, Jiangsu.

[3] Collecting Project Database.

Guangming Interview, November 20, 2013, Beijing: Materials stored in the Zhai

[2] Archives Office of CNPC.

of Appointment for new employee of CNPC in August 19, 1950, stored in the Letter

[1] _____

Deputy Director of the General Administration of Petroleum Management,

in the nation's capital, Beijing. Yan had recently been appointed as the

pioneering figures in the development of modern oil industry of China,

With the letter in hand, Zhai proceeded to meet Yan Shuang[3], one of the

With the letter in hand, Zhai proceeded to meet Yan Shuang[3]

to the front line of oil production.

Peking Union Medical College Hospital, waiting for a command to advance

They were assembled in a small building near the

institutions in China.[2]

Tsinghua University, Fudan University, and other prestigious academic college students assigned to Northwest China came from Peking University, search for oil, and a rallying call for him to go to the Northwest. The Corporation (CNPC). This event represented a curtain raiser for his lifelong which designated him as a new staff member of China National Petroleum Management, Ministry of Fuel Industry of the Central People's Government, by the Personnel Division of the General Administration of Petroleum signed

On August 19, 1950, Zhai received a letter of appointment[1]

goal he pursued with commitment and practical action.

and enhance its reputation on the global stage" became his life's mission, a

and perseverance in this field throughout his life. "Find oil for the country

jumping from a high diving platform. He exhibited remarkable dedication

university, he plunged into a demanding career in the oil industry like

his university studies despite numerous obstacles. Upon graduating from

Zhai Guangming experienced a challenging adolescence and completed

3.1 Going to the Northwest

48 2009, p. 45.

Century of Petroleum. Beijing: Petroleum Industry Press, August Writing Group.

[4] _____

in the construction of the country. He urged them to avoid falling behind,

oil. Yan encouraged all those present to go to the Northwest and participate

advanced equipment and an annual output of tens of thousands of tons of

stationed there. Out there was the largest oilfield in the country with the most

standard of living has been achieved by the geologists and oil workers

have been erected, various amenities have been installed, and a satisfactory

located beneath the Qilian Mountains. He noted that a few basic structures

In his address to the graduates, Yan observed that the oilfield was an asset

Fig. 3-1 Zhai Guangming's letter of appointment

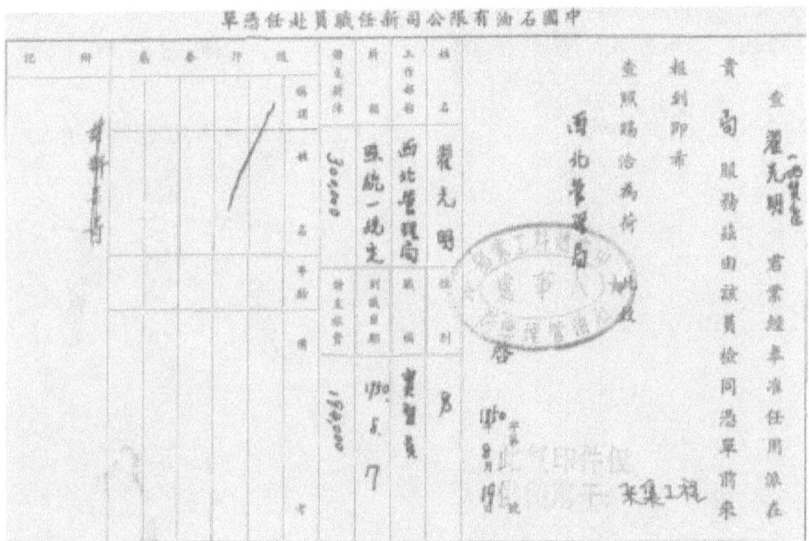

field.

working conditions of the workers in the oilfield and the construction of the

Northwest region, along with a comprehensive overview of the living and

detailed account of the dynamic oil exploration operations underway in the

in Beijing, Yan met with the newly graduated students and provided a

University in 1918, and was regarded as Zhai's predecessor. At a conference

had graduated from the Department of Mining and Metallurgy at Peking

He

effectively becoming the second leader of China's petroleum industry.[4]

Ministry of Fuel Industry (under the Central People's Government),

49 Ibid. [6] Collecting Project Database.

Guangming Interview, November 20, 2013, Beijing: Materials stored in the Zhai

[5]

and clanging on its tracks, playing the westbound overture. After a day and a

contentment. The train came to a stop and began to move again, swaying

from a customary demeanor of bitterness and sorrow to one of joy and

family. He then underwent a transformation in his emotional state, shifting

career, he was able to generate income to provide financial support for his

activities and search for oil deposits. Given that he had established his own

The objective of the journey to the Northwest was to engage in oil mining

and subsequently to Beijing, he had at last reached a pivotal point in his life.

including his college experience and relocations from Yichang to Tianjin

and a profound emotional state. Reflecting on the preceding twenty years,

contemplation, gazing out the window, immersed in a multitude of thoughts

During the journey, he sat in

first took a train from Beijing to Xi'an.[6]

With dreams and hopes, Zhai and his team headed for the Northwest. They with the significant undertaking of oil exploration.

alleviated, and he would be welcomed by a vast and promising world, along himself financially. The onerous responsibilities of daily life would soon be find himself no longer reliant on the charity of others and able to support experience a life of fulfillment and contentment. Zhai was also gratified to eager to contribute to the construction of the People's Republic of China to journey to the Northwest with great enthusiasm and anticipation. They were inspired Zhai Guangming and his fellow college students to embark on a The description of the oilfield by Yan was so vivid and appealing that it commitment to the college students.

any difficulties they faced, which was a testament to his dedication and in the oilfield directly to him. He also stated that he would assist them with He informed the students that they could report any issues they encountered oilfield immediately to begin the process of discovering the buried treasure. were determined to go to the Northwest, hoping that they would go to the

stated that the country required the services of all geology students who

keenly interested in recruiting individuals with expertise in geology. He

oil. As the senior official in charge of China's petroleum industry, Yan was

was then in urgent need of talents, as were the oilfields and the search for

The country

to refrain from desertion, and to take care on their journey.[5]

[7]-[9] Zhai Guangming Interview, November 20, 2013.

50

When they departed from Xi'an, it had already reached late fall. The climate

geology on site.

the inaugural contact with petroleum and the first lesson in petroleum

vital in his subsequent work at the forefront of exploration. It also marked

exploration. Although it was a rudimentary grasp of petroleum, it proved

region, Zhai acquired fundamental yet novel and crucial insights into oilfield

and permeability. At the transit station en route to the western mining

Additionally, they were introduced to new terminology, such as rock porosity

instruments employed for oil analysis, water analysis and lithology analysis.

and jars utilized for petroleum testing, as well as the core samples and

this laboratory that the graduates observed for the first time the bottles

It was in

experimenters and geologists of the Xi'an Preparatory Office.[191]

experimental procedures. This laboratory was established by the geological

was mainly used for the storage of core samples and execution of limited

The Xi'an Office was equipped with a modest laboratory facility, which

enduring friendship.

mutual support, assistance, and companionship, fostering a profound and

They provided

Bo-min, with whom he forged a strong bond of camaraderie.[8]

chance to become acquainted with Zhang Wei-ya, Zhang Xiao-yan, and Du

the personnel from the NPA who had been stationed in Xi'an. He also had the

20 days. During this period, Zhai had the opportunity to interact with most of

this timeframe. Zhai and his fellow graduates waited in Xi'an for more than

more than ten days to traverse the distance, with occasional delays exceeding

and the primary mode of transportation was heavy trucks, which often required

there was no rail service between Xi'an and Lanzhou. The roads were unpaved,

in the advancement of western oil Exploration & Development. At that time,

was the most important hub and transit station at the time. It played a pivotal role

oilfields. The office served as a vital nexus between Beijing and Lanzhou, and mainly provided lodging, transportation and other amenities for the personnel of

The Northwest Petroleum Administration (NPA) set up an office in Xi'an, which

waiting for transportation from Lanzhou.[7]

Xi'an, they had to wait for the order from Lanzhou, but in fact they were

which was the first stop on their westward journey and a transit station. In

night of a bumpy ride, a group of a dozen college graduates arrived in Xi'an,

[10]-[11] Zhai Guangming Interview, November 20, 2013.

with only the wind and sand for company. Soaking up the sunshine of

The journey was devoid of any cheerful melodies or expressions of joy,

undertaking in comparison to the subsequent field geology expeditions.

into the local environment. This was, of course, a relatively straightforward

Northwest, encountering the challenges of open-air travel and gaining insight

completed this arduous journey, Zhai experienced the winds and sands of the

Having

traditional heated brick bed common in northern China) at night.[11] (a

kang To ensure their safety and reduce expenditure, they slept on a large

package. Consequently, guests were required to bring their own bedding.

hotels at that time did not provide bedding as part of the accommodation

repeating this process four times. In contrast to the situation prevailing today,

travelers were required to descend and carry their belongings for the night,

in three days and four nights. Upon reaching each stopping point, the

resting at night. This approach allowed for the destination to be reached

manner similar to that described above, with the group traveling by day and

resembling that of a clay figure. Thus, the journey was undertaken in a

night, upon dismounting to repose, he was unidentifiable, his countenance

all the way, his face blue, his whole body covered in sand and dirt. Each

gripping the rope tightly for fear of rolling off. He was freezing and shivering

loaded with goods, and Zhai was positioned on the roof, not daring to move,

carriage was even more susceptible to this phenomenon. The truck was

The driver's cab was subject to significant airflow, and the roof of the

prevented one from opening one's eyes to take in the roadside views.

from its relentless fury. The constant presence of dust and grit in the air

against, and its erratic gusts resembled a marauder's raid, offering no respite

hurling minute particles of dust and sand that were impossible to shield

with no discernible presence for miles around. The wind howled persistently,

that seemed to cling to the truck as it bounced down the desolate landscape,

road extended in a seemingly endless ribbon, flanked by an eerie silence

moved like a snail, crawling on the bumpy dirt road in the Northwest. The

which was heavily laden and full to capacity. The vehicle

compartment,[110]

them, was situated in the driver's cab, while Zhai remained in the cargo

been confiscated from the KMT. Zhang Xiao-yan, who was traveling with

Beijing. Zhai and his fellow graduates rode in a Dodge truck that had

in the Northwest region of China was markedly more frigid than that of

www.ingramcontent.com/pod-product-compliance
Lightning Source LLC
Chambersburg PA
CBHW030113010526
44116CB00005B/228